The Mindful Approach to Working Life

A practical guide to enhancing wellbeing,
relationships, and performance at work

Catherine Midgley and Carroll Macey

ISBN No: 978.1.906542.97.9

Publishers: Barny Books
                   www.barnybooks.co.uk

Cover design by Stephanie Griffin

Contents

The Mindful Approach to Working Life

Introduction

Our intention in writing this book is to provide a useful and practical resource to enable you to be more effective at work by being more mindful. More than simply a book on mindfulness, it also contains some proven approaches and techniques designed to improve different aspects of what you do every day at work. The idea is for you to be able to pick the book up and get some guidance on specific issues you might be facing during the working day. It combines insight that we've gathered in our roles as leadership and management development consultants, and wisdom from our learning as mindfulness practitioners.

We have many years of work experience within organisations and working as consultants and coaches to organisations, public and private, large and small. We are acutely aware of the demands of the contemporary workplace and we and our clients have experienced the benefits of bringing mindfulness into our daily work.

The techniques in this book can help you to improve your wellbeing, relationships and overall performance through:

- Improving your focus
- Handling your emotions with greater ease
- Bringing more clarity to your decision making
- Interacting with colleagues more effectively
- Enhancing your communication style
- Bringing greater awareness and attention to meetings/emails/presentations etc.
- Leading and managing with a clearer intention and purpose

This book is designed so that you may choose to read it cover to cover, or just read chapters that are relevant and useful to you at a particular point in time. Some chapters will resonate with you more than others. For example, some chapters are specifically relevant if you manage people, so you may find it helpful to learn how to be a more mindful leader or carry out performance management processes in a more engaged way. Other chapters may be situation specific, e.g. you are experiencing some conflict or are feeling apprehensive about an upcoming presentation. Other chapters have broader appeal as topics that many of us face on a daily basis e.g. managing time effectively or having better quality conversations.

As you read through the book, you will notice there are similar, repetitive themes around how to be more mindful throughout the working day. This is deliberate for two reasons: Firstly, the approach to becoming more mindful is similar, whatever situation you are facing. Secondly, each chapter can be independently helpful by itself.

What is mindfulness? Jon Kabat-Zinn described it as, 'paying attention in a particular way: on purpose, in the present moment, and non-judgementally'. It's about noticing what's going on right now and developing the self-awareness to allow yourself to be more choiceful of your responses in the moment.

How mindful are you typically during the working day?

If you sometimes find yourself doing any of following, you have the potential to improve your mindfulness;

- Going through the day on 'auto-pilot'
- Getting distracted by thoughts about something that has happened or is yet to happen
- Reacting to something or somebody in a way that doesn't help the situation
- Condemning yourself or someone else for what has/hasn't happened
- Being in a meeting and your attention is elsewhere

We're not claiming that reading this book and acting on its ideas will prevent the above from happening 100% of the time. What we can say is it will help you to be more 'in the moment' more often. It will help you to pause more often so that you can check your thinking, check your responses before responding. It will help you to manage your own thinking so there is more acceptance and less judgement. Doing these things will promote and sustain your own wellbeing, enhance your relationships and improve your performance at work.

How to become more mindful

The suggestions we make throughout the book will start to make a difference if you apply them regularly. If you want to make a profound and sustained difference to how you feel, think and behave, this involves a deeper level of commitment to a daily practice of meditation.

Many people would like to be more mindful and experience the benefits of mindfulness without the discipline needed to develop the 'muscle' of mindfulness. You may appreciate the similarities between this and other goals such as losing weight, or getting fit.

There is no straightforward answer as to how long to meditate for each day or how long it takes before you notice a difference. It's as individual as we are. Any commitment to a daily practice is better than doing none. Ten minutes a day will help. If you have this as the foundation of your practice and then use some of the approaches we describe throughout the day, you are likely to start to notice a difference.

The idea is that the discipline of learning to focus your attention through a meditation practice is the training that can be integrated into daily life.

Your life at work and home will benefit hugely from a daily practice of both formal, informal and 'in-the-moment' mindfulness practice. Throughout the book we have given examples of how you can be more mindful during the working day.

By formal practice, we mean a regular time to sit and meditate, usually for at least ten minutes and often a longer practice will be more beneficial.

By informal practice, we mean completing your day-to-day activities in a mindful way i.e. mindful walking/driving/showering/working.

By 'in-the-moment' activities we mean shorter meditative practices, such as 'ten breaths' or the 'three step breathing space' which are helpful as 'top-ups' when needed.

Formal practice

At its most simple, meditation can be about settling down and following the breath. The challenge is to keep following the breath, and not the thoughts, ideas, concerns, memories etc. that can soon distract us from this simple practice.

A simple plan for formal practice:

Find a quiet place (not essential but highly desirable) where you are able to settle and either close your eyes or lower your gaze to a fixed spot in front of you.

Sit upright with your back slightly away from the back of the chair and your feet flat on the ground.

Notice the contact points with the chair and your body and take a settling breath.

Focus entirely on the sensation of the breath as you breathe in and out. Notice how your body moves in line with the breath.

Keep following the breath and continue this practice for at least ten minutes. The formal sessions can last as long as you like. Longer practices of 20 to 30 minutes often feel more beneficial.

Whilst you are following your breath you may become aware of your thoughts, feelings, and sensations in your body. As your thoughts appear, notice and acknowledge your thinking and then allow your thoughts to drift away. Now is not the time to get caught up in the thoughts with planning, ruminating or worrying. It's not the time to follow your thinking; it is the time to follow your breath. Avoid any judgement of yourself or your thinking. It is perfectly natural for our minds to generate thoughts, it's what minds do! The same for feelings and sensations, simply notice that they are there and let them go.

Informal practice

You have the opportunity to have moments of mindfulness throughout the day. This book invites you to be mindful when carrying out typical working activities or dealing with specific feelings that you experience at a particular point in time. You also have the opportunity to experience mindful moments at other times of the day when you simply bring all your attention to the activity you are doing at that time. The opportunities to be mindful are endless. Try focusing all your attention and engage all your senses as you:

- Get out of bed
- Clean your teeth
- Shower
- Eat breakfast
- Journey to work
- Sip your drink
- Taste your food
- Walk around
- Sit in your chair
- Stand
- Wash your hands
- Prepare food
- Wait at the coffee machine or water dispenser

Encourage your mind and body to be in the same place

In being mindful, you are encouraged to notice your thinking without following your line of thoughts. As you engage with informal mindfulness practices, you are likely to notice just how much thinking you do as your body is doing something else. Becoming more mindful means allowing ourselves to focus our attention on one thing at a time to gain the benefits that flow from focused and trained attention.

In-the-moment practice

In-the-moment practice can be used throughout the working day to allow you to clear your head, take stock and refocus.

Even a single, conscious breath, with focus and intention can enable you to pause in the moment, take stock and carry on with your day in a more mindful way.

We hope that you enjoy bringing mindfulness into your working life. Keep this book with you and refer to it when you need some practical guidance to be more mindful during your day to day activities at work. Using it regularly will help you form new habits that bring you greater balance and an improved sense of well-being.

At the end of each chapter is a summary of the key points for those moments when you quickly need to access a practice or remind yourself how to be mindful in particular situations.

More information on mindfulness practices is given in the appendix.

The Mindful Approach to

Starting the day well

How often do you arrive at work feeling calm, refreshed, energised and ready to focus mindfully on the day ahead? Or is the reality that you arrive at work frazzled by the journey to work, frustrated by uncooperative family members and feeling wound up about the day ahead and already stressed before the working day has begun? If you encounter any of these events in your daily morning routine then your mindful day at work needs to start from the moment you wake in order to optimise your chances of feeling calm, refreshed and energised. In this chapter we share with you some habits that will help you to start your day mindfully.

Upon waking

Take a moment to consider the first waking moments of each day. What thoughts run through your head? What feelings do you have? What physical sensations do you notice? Before you begin your normal, habitual routine, take a few moments to focus on the breath; pay attention to the passage of the breath into and out of your body. Bring your awareness to any thoughts, feelings and any physical sensations you have upon waking. Just notice, without judgement, whether they are positive or negative. As you observe your thoughts, feelings and physical sensations, simply label them, for instance, 'here's discomfort' or 'here's worry' or 'here's warmth' without becoming lost in following any subsequent thoughts or feelings. Gently return to the breath and when you are ready, prepare to get up. This whole process may only take a minute or two, or longer, as you wish.

As you step out of bed, be aware of your feet on the floor and how your body feels as you move from lying down to sitting to standing. Feel the floor beneath you and the texture of your flooring. As you are doing this you are simply allowing yourself to be in the present moment, with mind and body aligned.

Morning routine

Our daily routines enable us to do the activities we do every day without too much thought. These routines can be helpful in minimising the number of decisions we have to make. They can also be unhelpful in that we can get

11

stuck in a rut and do things without questioning if there is a better way. If you choose to bring more mindfulness to your morning routine, you will raise your levels of awareness of the present moment, allowing you to make more informed choices. It is also good practice in managing your mind to create higher levels of focus and engagement with your activities.

Start by noticing how 'in the moment' you are when you:

- Clean your teeth – do you always follow the same pattern? Do you notice the flavour of the toothpaste and how it feels in your mouth? Do you take time to notice how different your mouth feels before and after you've cleaned your teeth?
- Shower – do you notice the fragrance of the shower gel and the feel of the water on your skin? Do you wash your body in the same order without realising?
- Have your first drink of the day – do you really taste it? Do you notice the temperature as you swallow it down?
- Eat breakfast – do you notice the smell, the texture, the taste, the colours? Are you fully engaged in the eating experience as you would be if you were eating delicious food in a wonderful restaurant?
- Speak to others – how engaged are you in the conversations you're having? Do you take time to fully connect with those you live with?

Awareness of thoughts, feelings and sensations as you start your day

When you start your day mindfully you may start to realise how often you are physically doing one thing and your thinking is somewhere else entirely; maybe mulling over something that's happened or thinking over something that hasn't yet happened, planning for the day. These are important thinking skills and being mindful invites you to do these things with awareness and consciousness. Not being mindful of your thinking can lead to excessive mulling over of events that have happened or anticipating future events in a way that can cause anxiety.

We know it's not realistic to be fully mindful all the time. We are suggesting that you may benefit from increasing the number of occasions when you are fully present to what you are doing. When you are fully present, you are more likely to notice any tendencies to think back or think ahead in a way that is unhelpful. Once you're aware of this, you can do something about it.

Time to sit and breathe

If you are able to commit to taking some time each morning to sit and breathe with awareness, this will allow you some mental space in your morning routine. How much time you take is up to you, from a few conscious breaths to a meditation practice of ten to fifteen minutes or even longer. Simply sit with awareness and notice thoughts, feelings or physical sensations without processing these beyond observing them and allowing them to drift away.

The journey to work

However you get to work and however long it takes, you have opportunities to have mindful moments along the way. Tuning into these moments from time to time will allow you to reconnect to all the senses in your body, to separate you from your thoughts. This can help you become aware of any triggers that may be starting to create a stress response in you. These triggers might be challenging road conditions, delayed trains, crowded buses or tubes, inconsiderate drivers, bad weather etc. How much of your mental chatter is inwardly moaning and complaining about the journey and the challenges of the journey? How might this impact on your mood as you arrive at work?

Contrast this to a journey when you are simply present to whatever you are doing, aware of what's going on, without judgement, without complaint or criticism.

One way to create those moments of being present is to say to yourself, 'just driving', 'just travelling', 'just walking' etc. and really notice and take in all aspects of what's going on around you.

Imagine arriving at work calm, focused, with a sense of inner peace and energised for the day ahead.

Arriving at work

As you arrive at your place at work, do so with awareness, rather than on auto-pilot where you follow a daily routine without being aware of what you are doing or what is happening around you. Consider setting a goal to notice something new every day as you walk into the office. Notice your mood, notice your thoughts, notice your feelings, notice how you respond to colleagues as you arrive. Walk mindfully and be aware of your typical morning routine.

Most of us do the same thing every day. Check in with yourself how well your routine serves you in setting up a productive and fulfilling day. What habits could you challenge? If you could design a perfect start to the working day, what would this include? Connecting on a deeper level with your colleagues? Focusing clearly on the day ahead and your key priorities? Thinking about what behaviours will allow you the greatest impact and influence in an important stakeholder meeting? You may find that simply noticing what is here, now, enables you to give more effective feedback to your colleagues.

Settling into the day

As you sit down, grant yourself a few seconds to settle comfortably into your chair. Feel the connection between the chair and your body and your feet and the floor. Take three deep breaths and allow your mind to focus on the day ahead. Now you are ready to embrace the opportunities and challenges of the day with calmness, alertness and readiness.

Summary

- **Upon waking, breathe deeply and notice thoughts, feelings, sensations**
- **Bring awareness and attention to your morning routine**
- **Use your journey to work to practice acceptance and non-judgement**
- **Arrive at work and focus on being fully present**
- **Have the intention of having a mindful day**

The Mindful Approach to

A demanding day

Your head is buzzing; your focus is scattered; you feel a sense of overwhelm, maybe panic that things are getting out of control. The reality is that for the majority of working people for most of the time there is more to do than you can realistically cope with. There are many demands competing for your attention all the time. If, at some level you try to convince yourself that if you were more efficient you could cope with it all, you will always feel a sense of inadequacy and an inability to cope. In his book, *Busy. How to thrive in a world of too much*, Tony Crabbe says, 'Your job is not to control the demands made on you; it is to feel in control of your response to it'.

Regaining a sense of control

If you try to deal with all the demands that come your way, it's likely that your busy-ness has gone beyond stimulating to, 'not sure if I can cope with this'. You know you are not effective in this state of mind so rather than just ploughing on through the to-do list or rushing to the next meeting, take a moment to step off the treadmill. Notice, if your mind tries to convince you otherwise; 'I haven't got time to stop!' This is when you need to stop the most. It's time to re-gain a feeling of control.

Just sit; just walk; just breathe

Just stop, sit and place your feet flat on the ground. Feel the chair beneath you. Take a deep breath. Relax your shoulders. Unclench your jaw. Relax your hands in your lap. Allow your eyes to close or soften your gaze if you'd rather.

If you are walking, switch to mindful walking where you inhabit your body and your senses rather than your mind. Walk with awareness of your feet on the floor; engage your senses, walk purposefully and more slowly than normal.

Spend a minute just breathing and focusing on the breath going in and out of your body. Notice the thoughts of resistance that come into your mind. This is not the time to judge your thoughts, just to notice them. Mentally you can say to yourself, 'I notice that I'm thinking about *that report I have to write'/ that conversation I had with my boss / getting on with things rather than sitting here'*.....or whatever thoughts you observe.

During this process, you are slowing down and taking control of your thinking by not engaging with it, just seeing your thoughts as separate from you. You are not your thoughts.

Mindfulness is attention training and attention is best directed on one thing at once.

Once you've slowed down your thinking and regained a degree of mindful awareness, it's time to deal practically with the sense of overload.

Capture what's on your mind

The best way to deal with a busy mind is to capture your thinking in writing. This might be in the form of a list or mind-map, where you simply write down everything on your mind. Just write. Don't attempt to process it at this stage, just get it down on paper / on screen. This is not a to-do list; this is a list of everything that's on your mind and it might be work or home related.

Once you've captured everything that's on your mind, it's time to make a simple plan. Planning allows you to think forward in a mindful way and in doing so, reduce the weight of worries about things you have to do in the future. Once you have a plan in writing it's easier for the mind to be at rest because there's less concern about forgetting to do something. It gives a sense of control; a sense of being on top of things.

Ruthlessly prioritise

Prioritise according to how urgent and how important the items you have listed are. Notice any inner dialogue which is telling you it's ALL urgent or ALL important. Calmly decide which three items are **the** most urgent and **the** most important. These are your priorities. If any of these three things can be completed in two minutes or less, do it straight away. If the priorities have more than one step, identify the **first** step you ACTUALLY have to do to make progress. David Allen in his book *Getting Things Done* refers to this as a 'next action' and it has to be something that describes what you do i.e. 'arrange meeting' is not a 'next action' because it's not specific enough. 'Open Jo's online calendar', is a next action, as you can imagine yourself doing this.

Stay mindful throughout the prioritisation process; notice your thinking; be in the moment and focus your attention fully on your planning.

Once you've identified the top three actions, choose the next three. Pay attention to prioritising what's really important rather than just doing things that are urgent but actually not that important. Decide when you will tackle the priorities. Schedule them into your calendar so that you are reminded what needs doing, when.

Do you _have_ to do this/do _you_ have to do this?

Be ruthless about challenging whether things on your list need to be done by you or need to be done at all. Are there meetings you can excuse yourself from? Are there jobs you can delegate? Notice any 'shoulds' or 'musts' in your internal dialogue and challenge them gently. For example, you might hear yourself saying, 'I'm the only one who can do this - If I don't do this, it won't get done to my satisfaction'. Tune into your thoughts and offer a considered challenge: 'What makes me think this? Do I have any evidence of this? Who else could possibly do this? How could I support them to ensure standards are achieved?' This pattern of thinking takes you away from the auto-pilot habitual reaction and allows you to think things through mindfully and come up with a considered response.

Once you have engaged your attention and focused on your action plan for the future, check in with how you are feeling and the extent to which you have a greater feeling of control. Once you are making conscious choices about doing what's important and equally consciously deciding what **not** to do, you are back in control and mastering your feelings of overwhelm.

Summary

- **Give yourself time to regain a feeling of control**
- **Align your mind and body through breathing/sitting/walking with body/mind awareness**
- **Write down everything that's on your mind**
- **Identify your top three priorities**
- **Consider dropping or delegating activities with mindful awareness of the implications**
- **Be aware of your inner dialogue and how it directs your actions**

The Mindful Approach to

Regulating your emotions

The emotions people experience at work have a profound effect on them directly and on those around them. If you are to be effective at work, you need to feel comfortable expressing emotions and also in managing the expression of emotions.

This chapter helps you to focus on becoming aware of your own emotions as you experience them and managing those emotions in a helpful way.

Take time daily to sit and be mindful

Ongoing mindfulness practice will help you to regulate your emotions more effectively; it's one of the benefits experienced by people who regularly practice mindfulness. A daily practice of sitting and breathing, allowing thoughts and emotions to arise, be acknowledged and then drift away without judgement or engagement teaches you to understand and manage your emotions more fully.

What do you learn as you practice?

- To **observe** your thoughts and emotions: observing involves noticing events as they occur in the present moment
- To **describe:** describing involves being able to label present moment events with short words or phrases
- To **accept** without judgement: acceptance encourages an attitude of openness and curiosity and refers to the ability to refrain from evaluating or trying to change events

Increasing awareness of your emotions

The practice of sitting mindfully will enhance your emotional awareness. How aware are you of the emotions you have experienced today? This is the first stage of being able to manage your emotions; to become aware of them. As you focus on becoming more mindful, the more aware you are likely to be of the vast range of positive and negative emotions you experience during the day. These different emotions can range from a momentary flash of anger/frustration/pleasure/hope etc. to a full blown emotional outburst or ongoing positivity and joy. Our focus here is on managing negative emotions as these are the ones with the potential to cause damage both personally and professionally. It is important to note that we cannot know sadness unless we have known joy and vice versa.

As you go through the day, actively start to notice your emotions. As you do so, start to label those emotions e.g. 'anxiety', 'fear', 'frustration', 'anger' etc. Labelling them in this way keeps your distance from these emotions which encourages you to see them as being separate from yourself rather than part of you.

The emotional source

Our emotional experience can be:

- A reaction to something external e.g. being criticised, being ignored, a poor performance rating

- A reaction to something internal, often our own thoughts e.g. embarrassment at an inappropriate comment, anxiety about a forthcoming meeting

Notice what triggers the emotional response in you and also be aware that although you are not able to control the external event and stop it happening, you can control your interpretation of it and your response to it. The management of internal triggers is also within your control. This grants us extraordinary power over our thoughts and emotions.

Coping in the moment

To access our power and control over our emotions, we need to keep our distance from the in-the-moment emotional reaction. Labelling how we are feeling helps us with this and then we have the opportunity to let go of these thoughts. This is especially helpful if the source of the emotion is internal and at that point in time, no-one else is involved.

A shift to a more rational frame of mind can be powerful in changing the feeling. Ask yourself if you want these feelings, these thoughts, this reaction. Is how you are reacting helping the situation? This is not so easy to do in a moment when you feel you are being provoked. A deep breath, a moment to relax your body can help you to channel your emotions to a more considered response.

- Pause
- Breathe
- Notice what's going on; internally, externally, the big picture
- Respond in a way that helps the situation

Reflect to learn from experience

You have the opportunity to learn after every experience of an emotional reaction. Reflect on how you handled it and how you could do better next time. It's useful to consider what provoked the reaction (especially if this was a reaction to a person or a situation) and try to identify what was behind your emotional response – had one of your values been crossed? If you're thinking, for instance, 'that's not fair!' 'that's not true!' a values clash may be in evidence. If you're thinking, 'that was stupid!' 'how could you say that?' some judgement is in evidence. A mindful approach is helpful to invite a spirit of curiosity rather than disapproval or judgement.

A helpful set of questions to reflect on is:
- What am I really reacting to here?
- Am I jumping to conclusions?
- Is there another way of dealing with this?
- Is it fact or opinion?
- How might somebody else see this situation?
- How important will it be six months from now?

Managing your thinking

An important tool in regulating your emotions is to manage your thinking. This means becoming aware of what you are thinking, challenging your thinking and moving on from unhelpful thinking patterns. Thoughts are not reality, they are mental events and are more often about ruminating on past events or thinking about future ones. A mindful approach invites you to identify unhelpful thoughts and invites you not to get caught up in them. Challenging your thinking using the questions above allows you to take control and find more constructive ways of responding.

Knowing yourself well, acting with awareness, in the moment, and a regular commitment to develop these skills through mindfulness practice will help you express your emotions authentically in a way that is helpful to yourself and others.

Summary

- **Take time to meditate daily**
- **Label emotions and observe them as transitory**
- **Recognise the emotional trigger**
- **Pause, breathe and respond with awareness**
- **Learn from your experiences**

The Mindful Approach to

Stressful situations

What do you do when you are having one of those days when things just never seem to go the way that you planned? Perhaps you are about to leave the office for an important meeting and your car keys are nowhere to be found, or you need to locate a file so that you can finish that important piece of work and no matter which folder you look in you just can't find it. Or perhaps it is in the midst of a team meeting when emotions are running high, people are talking over each other and no agreement is being reached. These are the times when a mindful approach is most needed and often the hardest to access.

Emotional hijack

At any of these moments, our ability to respond rationally can be hijacked by emotions such as frustration, anger, fear, impatience and a host of others. When this happens, our feelings are heightened and our behaviours may be disproportionate to the situation. This is called an amygdala hijack. It is a biochemical reaction by a part of your brain called the amygdala that perceives a situation as a threat, sends a signal to your body to get ready to fight or run away. There are three things that are important to know about amygdala hijacks:

- They are instantaneous. Within a moment, you react to the perceived threat
- They are non-rational. You brain decodes the situation as a threat and needs you to react accordingly
- The reaction that it triggers is no different to how you'd be if faced by an attacker, but the attacker is not real

The way that you react in stressful situations is probably a habitual pattern of behaviour. Whether you shout, cry, feel depressed and are overwhelmed it is likely that you have a well-trodden path in your neural networks that says when X happens, do Y! So, something happens, a trigger, and you react automatically.

Regaining control

If you are on auto pilot then you are more likely to react in an emotional, out of control way. Your head may be full of noise, (Where did I put...? Why do I always...? Why has this happened now?) and your body is full of feelings. There is no space for focus and clarity; no space to be still and to allow you to find the missing item/solve the problem etc.

What you need to do is metaphorically press the Reset button!

Self-awareness

In that moment of out-of-control, emotional reaction, the first step is to gain self-awareness.

Stop. Pause. Notice. Take a breath.

Notice how you are feeling and thinking.

Bring your focus into your body and take conscious breaths. Notice how you feel, physically and mentally. Just notice. Don't make any attempt to change your experience. Pay attention to your breathing and follow the breath as you breathe in and out.

As thoughts come in notice them and let them go as you return your attention to your breath.

As this happens, you move from emotional reaction to a greater sense of being in control; you are more able to think clearly. Focus on your goal, whether it's find your keys/file or bring about a change of behaviours in the team meeting and take action based on a more mindful perspective, calmer and more rational in your approach.

Surf the waves

When you are emotionally hijacked, focusing on the breath is an anchor to the present moment. Even a few, conscious breaths will help stop the body's natural reaction of flight or fight and enable you to bring focus, clarity and a different perspective into the moment. This enables you to think more calmly and rationally so that you can overcome the sense of panic that can prevail during an amygdala hijack. Jon Kabat-Zinn said, 'You can't stop the waves, but you can learn to surf'.

Practise following the breath a few times a day, when you're feeling calm. Then, when you need to surf the waves of an emotional challenge, you'll have already built your skills.

Reducing emotional hijacks

The approach we've shared above can help you deal with those 'in-the-moment' loss of control occasions. What's even better than dealing with them as they arise is reducing the number of times that you have to face the 'hijack' scenario in the first place. A more mindful approach reduces the occasions when the keys or file are misplaced. A more mindful team is less likely to be talking over one another. The deeper the foundations of mindfulness you build into your everyday lives, the less you are likely to experience those 'losing it' moments. This means a commitment to regularly building your awareness through focusing on the breath for at least ten to fifteen minutes a day. This means taking regular pauses throughout the day where you consciously become more mindful of what is going on in you and around you at that time. Everyday mindfulness connects you more deeply to what's going on for yourself and others, and as such, reduces those times which trigger a hijack and cause unwanted and unhelpful emotions and behaviours.

Summary

In the moment:

- **Stop! Focus on your breath**
- **Notice what you are feeling**
- **Return your attention to the breath for ten breaths**
- **Address the situation mindfully**

The Mindful Approach to

Conversations

How many of your conversations do you fully engage in where your attention is completely focused on the other person? Conversations where you are watching and listening intently, where you are engaged in understanding their perspective and sharing your own, not being distracted by anything going on in the environment nor in your own head? Conversations where you are fully present? If these are the type of conversations you have daily at work then congratulations! We're betting the quality of your side of the interaction, at least, is excellent! You are likely to be known as someone who's a great listener, who's able to understand the other person's perspective and put your own across in a way that engages others.

What makes a mindful conversation?

Mindful conversations will happen where both people talking are fully present to one another; where there's a real connection and understanding between you. Where you notice your own thoughts and feelings but don't get caught up in them. The environment could be in a meeting or one to one or at the drinks machine. Even if you are the only one being mindful in the interaction, the quality of your listening and the quality of your response will be such that the whole level of the conversation will be raised.

Creating the conditions for mindful listening

A mindful conversation starts with the intention to be focused on the other person and the conversation; this means minimising distractions, such as phone/laptop/tablet/other people wherever possible. Being mindful means dedicating your time to the conversation and focusing your attention. You are creating the environment for meaningful connection if you manage the distractions to the best of your ability.

With the intention, the environment and the focus in place, the next step is to make an appropriate level of eye contact i.e. not staring at them, nor failing to look at them. Be observant and notice how you feel as a result of what you see. Look for clues on what's not being said by the other person.

Listen carefully to how the other person speaks; how much emotion is in their voice? What might that emotion say about how they are feeling? Notice what you pick up as an observer of your thoughts about them. It's important that you are able to understand and empathise with the other person and also important that you are able to retain some emotional distance to allow objectivity.

The challenge in having a mindful conversation is not getting caught up in any external or internal distractions when your mind wanders away from the present-moment experience of the interaction.

Your mind will wander; the more mindful you are, the quicker you will be able to notice when your mind does wander and you will be more able to allow your attention to return to what's being said rather than focusing on the contents of your wandering mind.

Your purpose in listening is to understand the other person and mindfulness invites you to seek this understanding without judgement or criticism.

Speaking mindfully

Once the other person has finished speaking, be conscious of what you are about to say and the impact it might have. Perhaps speak a little more slowly and carefully and choose your words with care because they can have a positive or negative impact the moment they are out your mouth. The more carefully you speak, the less likely you are to use 'filler' noises like 'ums' and 'errs' or words like, 'you know' on a regular basis.

Be aware of your choice of words through inner questioning, 'Is it helpful?' 'Is it true?' 'Does it add to the conversation?' Think about your own tone of voice and body language as you speak and ensure that your voice and body are consistent with the message you are putting across.

When you have a difficult message to deliver

It can be especially difficult to be mindful if you have negative feedback or bad news to share. In these instances, our minds can project a number of scenarios about how the person may react and these projections can diminish our effectiveness in having the conversation. When we learn to stay present in the moment, we can see how the person is reacting and adjust our response accordingly. Remember that our thoughts are simply mental events and not the reality.

As you speak, stay mindful of how the other person is responding; ensure that you don't react too quickly. Notice any desire within yourself to speak in defensiveness or judgement or dismissal. Take a moment to tune into what the other person is saying, pause as you breathe and then respond with consideration of the impact on the other person.

Handling emotions

Is there a place for emotion in mindful conversations? Absolutely. Is there a place for losing emotional control? No. If this happens, chances are your autopilot responses have taken over and you are no longer responding in the present but are likely re-running an old pattern of behaviour that you have used previously. Notice your own emotional response and label it mentally e.g. frustration/anger/upset/anxiety. As you do so, you are being more objective about the feeling and therefore equipping yourself to handle that feeling more effectively by creating some distance between you and the emotion.

Phone calls and conference calls

These can be more challenging than face to face conversations as you don't have the visual clues that face-to-face affords you, and the temptations to multi-task are stronger because the other person can't see you. You may find yourself on the phone but sending an email. Or on a conference call but half-listening to a conversation elsewhere in the office. These are everyday occurrences that undermine your commitment to a mindful conversation. Notice the temptation to multi-task. We convince ourselves that we will be more productive: In reality the conversation will be less effective as your attention is scattered. The quality of whatever else you're focused on will be compromised too. Notice your distraction and bring your attention back to the other person in the conversation and deepen your connection with them.

Full attention and full engagement

Mindful conversation is about engaging all your senses fully in listening and speaking and noticing any internal or external distractions that pull you away from that deep connection. When you notice your mind wandering and following a path away from deep listening and considered responses, gently bring your attention back to the other person and how you are engaging with them.

Summary

- **Focus your attention on the other person**
- **Minimise internal and external distractions**
- **Look and listen attentively to better understand**
- **Manage your wandering mind**
- **Choose your words with care**
- **Notice the verbal and non-verbal responses**
- **Manage your own response**
- **Mentally label any of your negative emotions**
- **Focus only on the conversation; avoid multi-tasking**

The Mindful Approach to

Difficult colleagues

If we asked you to think of one or two people whose behaviour you find challenging, chances are you would be able to suggest a couple of names! People who you might consider to be unreasonable, frustrating, negative, anxious, irritating, domineering etc. Others may agree with your assessment or it might be only you who experiences this individual in this way. Some people may even see you as 'difficult'. This chapter will help you deal with such colleagues in a mindful way, recognising we have limited ability to influence a complete change in their behaviour.

Think about the behaviours of your 'difficult' colleague

Take some time to reflect on the colleague or colleagues whose behaviour you find challenging and identify what is it about their behaviour that affects you. Look at it purely from a factual basis at first; what are the observable behaviours in the colleague? Refrain from judging their behaviours as mindfulness is a practice of non-judgement. Just identify the facts. Then ask yourself what story you are telling yourself about these facts.

For example, a colleague may consistently dominate meetings, speak over others, and not give others a chance to speak. What is the internal dialogue in your head? 'Loves the sound of his own voice... always has to be right... aggressive tone.... thinks no-one else has any good ideas...'

Your response in the moment

The tendency here might be to react, either internally when you effectively stop listening and get caught up in your own thoughts about the individual or you may speak out, attacking the individual. The mindful approach suggests you notice what's going on for you emotionally in this moment. Identify and acknowledge the emotion you are experiencing, e.g. I am starting to feel angry/frustrated. Allow yourself to witness what you are feeling, rather than getting caught up in what you are feeling. Realise that your emotions are temporary and that this feeling will pass. Once you are feeling calm, now is the time to decide if and how to intervene. From a place of calm, you avoid reactivity, and instead ask yourself, 'How would I act here at my best?' Your decision might be to speak out in the moment, with consciousness and awareness or to resolve to say nothing and speak later to the individual about how you experienced their behaviour. Or you may choose to say nothing as that may be the right thing to do; the important thing is, whatever you decide, it's a conscious, rational decision rather than a default choice.

Seeing it from their perspective

It's also important to try to understand the perspective of the person whose behaviour you find difficult. What's going on for them? In what way might their behaviour make sense to them? What are they hoping to achieve? What are they afraid of? And here's a tough question to ask yourself - in what way might I be responsible for this behaviour?

The mindful response

A mindful approach invites compassion and acceptance; this doesn't mean that we don't try to help people change and we don't offer feedback; it simply means when we do intervene, we do so with awareness, understanding and compassion for the person, even if their behaviour is unacceptable.

There is always the opportunity to learn from how we respond to others; when someone triggers us, it's usually an indication that we have to learn something about ourselves. It's like they hold up a mirror that allows us to reflect on an aspect of ourselves that may need some work. Even if we are unable to effect a change on their behaviour, we can ask ourselves how we can learn from the situation.

Taking time to listen and deepen your understanding

One practical way to deal with difficult behaviour is to take time to listen to the individual; to understand their perspective as fully as possible; to offer them feedback in terms of the impact of their behaviour and agree what needs to happen to enable you both to work effectively together. This might mean agreeing that you both need to make some changes. Sometimes, if you find someone difficult to work with, they may find you difficult to work with too. It may be that your personalities are too similar; it may be that your personalities are entirely different; both can lead to challenges.

Accepting your colleague

If your colleague is unable or unwilling to change his/her behaviour, or if you feel unable to broach the subject with them, then the only option is to accept the person and the situation and manage things such that the impact on you is minimised. Limit time you spend with them as far as possible. When you are in their company, work on staying calm and on practicing non-judgement. This means being non-judgemental of them and their behaviour and of yourself, you may find this practice challenging!

A message of loving kindness

You may also find it helpful to practice words of 'loving-kindness', a silent inward repetition of loving kindness directed inwardly to yourself, to those you love and in this instance, to the colleague whom you find challenging

May I be filled with loving kindness

May I be peaceful and at ease

May I be well

May I be safe

May I be happy

May he/she be filled with loving kindness

May he/she be peaceful and at ease

May he/she be well

May he/she be safe

May he/she be happy

As you gently repeat this internally, notice how you respond when offering your challenging colleague loving kindness, peace, ease, health, safety and happiness. Notice it, let it pass, and focus on the internal words you are speaking. Reciting these words inwardly helps us to be more compassionate and understanding of our colleague as a fellow human who may well be troubled in some way; if we are unable to help them to change, at least this enables us to work towards acceptance of the person and the situation.

Summary

- **Observe your colleague's behaviours in a non-judgemental way**
- **Notice your own inner emotional reaction to this colleague**
- **Be understanding of their perspective; listen to them**
- **Respond as you would do at your best**
- **Be accepting of your colleague**
- **Wish yourself and them well through the 'loving kindness' approach**

The Mindful Approach to

Conflict

It almost sounds like a contradiction in terms — surely if everyone was mindful, there would be very little conflict? There's a truth in this; the more mindful we are, the less likely we are to reactively engage in conflict. Conflict is when there's an interaction involving differences in perspective, beliefs, actions or interests. Not all conflict is unhealthy, having different points of views can create new approaches and perspectives. The type of conflict that we are talking about here is when the nature of conflict is such that emotions tend to run high and damage can be done to relationships; a mindful approach can help regulate emotions and preserve relationships.

Approaches to conflict

There can be reasons for fearing conflict such as: fear of rejection; loss of relationships; being seen as selfish; hurting someone; saying the wrong thing. As you're reading this you can probably think of your own reasons why you might fear conflict. A well-known tool for analysing the ways that you would typically approach conflict is called the Thomas Kilman Inventory (TKI). After completing the questionnaire, you are given an assessment of your typical response to conflict based on five positions determined by your level of assertiveness and cooperativeness. The five positions are:

- **Competing** - Assertive and uncooperative - When you go all out to achieve your objectives at the expense of others
- **Accommodating** - Unassertive and cooperative — When you do your best to meet others needs at the expense of your own
- **Avoiding** - Unassertive and uncooperative — When you avoid the issue entirely
- **Collaborating** - Assertive and cooperative — When you work together with others to actively find a solution that meets both of your needs
- **Compromising** - Moderately assertive and moderately competitive — When both parties work towards a solution by each giving up part of what they want

It is important to remember that no one position is better than another as your response is dependent on the situation. When the way that you are responding is not working for you, noticing the mode you are in raises your awareness of choice of response.

How do you respond to conflict?

Think about your own preferred ways of dealing with conflict – these might vary from circumstance to circumstance depending on how much power and influence you believe you and the other person have and how important the issue is to you.

Let's imagine you're in a meeting when someone says something that makes you feel angry or uncomfortable. Notice that feeling in yourself. Notice what happens in your body and notice what happens in your mind. Pay attention to any judgements that might spring to mind, for instance;

- You are ignoring what I want here
- You don't understand me
- What a stupid idea
- That's not fair
- That's an irresponsible thing to say

Being choiceful

Notice how you may instinctively want to react:

To compete/accommodate/avoid/collaborate/compromise. So at this stage you become an observer to your own thoughts and feelings and proposed actions. Now you're in a position to choose the most appropriate response, which will depend on the circumstances and the context.

In most instances, a response which validates the other person's feelings (even if you don't agree with them) will be helpful; an acknowledgement of their feelings enables them to feel better understood. Conflict grows with the absence of understanding so an emphasis on trying to understand the other person tends to reduce the emotions of conflict.

Make a conscious decision to manage your response here by pausing and taking a breath. Mindfulness invites us to avoid judgement of the other person (and here, we're talking about any kind of labelling of the other person being unreasonable, demanding, ridiculous, unfair etc.) by simply noticing our thoughts towards the other person and choosing not to get caught up in them. You can imagine that if you label the other person in a negative way, it's easier to justify any negative behaviour on your part.

Be mindful also of your body language; be conscious of relaxing your face, shoulders and hands. Focus your attention on releasing the tension from your body.

As you heighten your levels of mindfulness in the moment, you are better able to choose the level of assertiveness and the level of cooperation required to resolve the situation. It's best to be flexible in your approach to conflict resolution, depending on the context, how important the issue is, the power dynamics of the situation, the relationship with the other person etc. You may choose any of the approaches outlined above (competing, accommodating, avoiding, collaborating, compromising) depending on the situation.

Which approach to use, when

Use the **competing** style when quick, decisive action is essential (e.g. emergencies) and when you are the expert and you know you are right. Be conscious that this style can damage relationships when over-used and if you tend to think you always know better than others.

Use the **accommodating** style if the issue is not of great importance to you or the relationship you have with the individual is far more important than the issue under discussion. Be aware that if you are dealing with a more competitive colleague, you may be taken advantage of if they know you will often back down.

Use the **avoiding** style to allow other people to calm down or when you know that engaging in conflict is potentially counter-productive. Be aware of how others may perceive this style as a lack of willingness to face issues.

Use the **collaborating** style when it's important to take both perspectives into consideration and you are prepared to put the effort in to work together to reach agreement. There are no specific downsides to using the collaborative style and it's often a helpful one which can be facilitated by using a calming response such as 'I hear your concerns/frustration/perspective... so let's take a look at this together to see if we can resolve the issues you've identified'.

This approach changes the conflict situation from a 'you vs me' to an 'us vs the problem'.

Use the **compromising** style when you are under time pressure and it's a convenient way to reach agreement or when you need a back-up plan when a collaborative approach hasn't worked. Sometimes the compromise approach can leave both sides feeling less than satisfied as neither has quite got what they wanted.

Responding appropriately

It's helpful to use 'I' rather than 'you' language. Avoid expressions like 'you should' or generalisations such as 'you always' as these can provoke an angry and defensive reaction.

Keep listening, keep speaking with awareness and keep observing what's going on inside you and for the other person. Keep in mind your intention for the interaction.

If view-points are polarised and emotions are running high, focus on uncovering any common ground. Explore what is really important to the other person and then share what's important to you.

In most instances at work, it is important to maintain the relationship with the other person and it's also important to get your objectives met. This requires a fine balance between listening, understanding and asserting your own position. Be flexible, open and yet persistent and recognise when you need to change your perspective and when you need to push ahead with your own agenda.

As we mentioned earlier, not all conflict is unhealthy and engaging in appropriate and moderate amounts of mindful conflict can be hugely beneficial in the workplace; it can lead to stronger relationships and improved outcomes. It can fuel individual, team and organisational performance. The nature of today's workplace often presents us with frequent opportunities to develop our skills of mindfulness, so look out for the next opportunity to deal with conflict in a more mindful way.

During a conflict situation you can also draw on the chapter on The Mindful Approach to Conversations (Page 25), as your effectiveness during a conflict situation depends on you being able to listen mindfully and being able to focus on the other person without getting caught up in your own thoughts and feelings.

Summary

- **Develop awareness of different approaches to conflict**
- **Notice your own internal response**
- **Choose your response with care and with respect**
- **Use 'I' language, stay calm, open and non-judgemental**

The Mindful Approach to

Managing upwards

One of the most important relationships at work is the one you have with your boss. A great boss will motivate, support, challenge and develop you; a poor one can cause stress, frustration and anxiety. Without doubt, it's a relationship worth nurturing and to do so with mindfulness will help you build an effective working relationship with more awareness, more compassion and more understanding.

Understanding your boss

The starting point for building a healthy working relationship with your boss is to understand as fully as possible what's important to him/her; what are his/her work goals and personal aspirations? What pressures is he/she under? Professional or personal? What's your boss's preferred way of working? Big picture or detail? How much involvement does your boss like to have? What does your boss need to/like to know? What are your bosses strengths and weaknesses?

Understanding yourself

It's equally important to be able to have the same level of self-awareness with regards to yourself, as the other partner in this relationship. A candid appraisal of your own goals/motivations/strengths/weaknesses and of your preferred ways of working enables you to see yourself with more objectivity, from an observer's perspective. A key part of mindfulness is being able to observe your own thoughts, feelings and behaviours without getting caught up in what's going on. This exercise enables you to practice this aspect, along with the need for non-judgement of what you uncover.

Proactively using understanding to develop the relationship

As you carry out this assessment, notice any similarities and differences between you and your boss. This will enable you to spot any potential areas of conflict. For example you may just want to communicate from a top line perspective, whereas your boss may want more detail. Notice how you feel when you identify areas of difference. Does this provoke any emotional feelings in you? Any judgement? Be an observer of these feelings in yourself as they may help you identify potential areas of conflict.

As well as any likely challenges to the relationship, you will also be able to identify positive factors that can potentially enhance the relationship with your boss. With this information, you are in a position to build a relationship that meets both sets of needs/wants as far as possible.

Be prepared to be flexible in the way you work with your boss; ultimately it's easier for you to adapt to his/her way of working than influencing your boss to adapt to yours!

The more open you are about agreeing expectations of one another, the more you are likely to build the foundation for a successful relationship. It's helpful to agree all expectations up front to avoid surprises further down the line.

Mindfully managing the relationship

Allow yourself some time to reflect on your relationship with your boss and focus on the breath as you do so. What thoughts emerge? What feelings? What physical sensations in the body? This enables you to view your relationship through the lens of mindfulness and surfaces any issues, assumptions, expectations and judgements. It's important to remember that your thoughts are just thoughts; just mental events, not reality. Know also that these thoughts and feelings will influence your behaviour towards your boss.

Take a fresh perspective

Many relationships can run on 'auto-pilot' almost to a pre-determined script of familiarity with the implicit agreement of both parties. With conscious awareness that mindfulness encourages, look at the relationship afresh. Use the knowledge you have gained from better understanding yourself, your boss and the relationship between you to approach each new interaction from a position of curiosity and compassion, understanding and most importantly, being non-judgemental. Be very present to what he/she is saying; be very present to your own stream of thoughts and look for ways to build a healthy relationship.

Seek to understand the intentions behind your boss's questions and comments; recognise that they have their own frailties and blind-spots. Work to build trust with your boss through your performance and your behaviour. Sometimes this will mean challenging your boss's expectations, not from a position of defensiveness, but from a realistic assessment of what's achievable. Ensure your boss knows and believes your commitment, both to them/your goals and the organisation. See things from your boss's perspective and be prepared to share your own.

Seek out your boss's strengths

If you already have a strong relationship with your boss, it's easy to see and value their strengths. If your relationship is poor, noticing and acknowledging strengths might be more challenging to do, yet it is critical to your relationship to be able to do this. What has helped them to progress to their current position? What could you learn from them? What do other people recognise as their strengths? Answering these questions from a position of honesty and curiosity will help ensure you have a broader perspective of their abilities. Look for opportunities to offer them feedback regarding their strengths in your joint interactions. Sincere and heartfelt recognition of your boss's strong points encourages a positive relationship and may lead to a reciprocation of strengths-spotting on their part too.

Focus on joint goals

Relationships thrive on joint goals; where there's alignment, there's a joint sense of direction and purpose. Having reflected on your boss's goals, you know what his/her priorities are; be aware that by default, these are best considered to be your priorities too. Mismatched priorities are likely to lead to conflict; aligned priorities can create and sustain jointly supportive endeavours, where you work from the same perspective to achieve shared objectives. Notice any internal resistance you encounter to this. You may not think that your boss has the right priorities; you may not like the idea of supporting your boss's priorities. Whatever thoughts you observe, simply notice them, without judging them and focus on your intention to create a positive working relationship with your boss.

Invest in the relationship

The more you commit to following the ideas above, the less likely there is to be conflict. If you do have a difference of opinion, this is the time to handle it mindfully (see The Mindful Approach to Conflict Page 33). Ultimately, it's up to you to work at the relationship by noticing and acting on what nurtures that relationship and what depletes it. The relationship can best be managed through setting the right intentions, being open to experiencing how it is and by working to create an authentic and effective relationship which supports the needs of the organisation, yourself and your boss.

Summary

- **Focus on understanding, rather than judging, your boss**
- **Build self-awareness and notice similarities/differences**
- **Give time and energy to building the relationship**
- **Notice strengths and acknowledge these**
- **Align priorities**

The Mindful Approach to

Team Working

Patrick Lencioni, author of *Overcoming the Five Dysfunctions of a Team* states in his book, 'teamwork remains one sustainable competitive advantage that remains largely untapped'.

To what extent is your team fully functional, really harnessing the strengths and synergy of the collective, focused on the common goal? How much more could your team achieve if each member was fully committed to the success of the team's objectives and saw the development of the team being critical to this success?

Let's consider a team that works together mindfully: A team where each member truly listens to one another. A team that remains focused on shared objectives. A team that is able to come to decisions quickly, problem-solve effectively, change direction with flexibility. A team that talks openly and manages conflict without fear. A team that operates mindfully is far more likely to achieve these outcomes than a team where each individual has insufficient awareness of their moment to moment experience and how they impact others.

Developing a mindful team perspective

Take a moment to choose to focus on the now. Start to be present in the moment by focusing on your breath. It is so easy to get caught up in all the activity, relationships, decisions, tasks, and project deadlines that need to be met. It is simple but not easy to step out for a few minutes and observe without judgement what is happening for you and with your team members. Choose, for a moment, to still the inner chatter of your mind by focusing on your breath. The breath is an anchor to the present moment. Resting your attention on the path of the breath allows you to gain focus and clarity.

Think about your own team and how you feel about being a member of that team. Think about your fellow team members and how you feel about each of them. Think about your own contribution to the team vs how others contribute. How do your thoughts and feelings impact on your interactions with your team members? How aware are you of the values/wants/needs/challenges of each team member? What are the dynamics like in your team?

As you contemplate the questions above, pay attention to how your awareness and understanding develops.

Noticing your inner dialogue

Greet your inner dialogue with curiosity. Maybe

... you are anxious about how you are perceived in the team

... you are careful not to rock the boat

... your voice dominates in the team

... you drown out quieter team members

... you typically dismiss the perspective of certain team members

... you are overly influenced by certain dominant members

Note your own responses, without judgement, just noticing what is. Now consider how your inner dialogue affects the interactions within the team and your commitment to team objectives. To what extent do your own thoughts and feelings help or hinder the team dynamic?

Create space to reflect through focusing on the breath and bring your awareness to these questions:

Ask yourself:

Trust – Do you trust your team? Do your team members trust each other?

When trust exists in teams, weaknesses and mistakes are shared openly. People ask for help and are not afraid of tapping into each other's skills and experiences; feedback is sought and given and there are no grudges held. In order to build trust, people need to be willing to open up about themselves. How well do your team know each other? What is important to them personally? How many siblings do they have? What is their proudest achievement so far in their life outside of work? What has been their most challenging time? Sharing these facts about your lives helps to create bonds between people.

If you understand the events that shape a person, it's easier to connect with them. You'll be less likely to be judgemental of them or their actions. It's harder to let a person or the team down when the dynamic is more personal. At the next team meeting, find a way of inviting each member to share something about themselves that the rest of the team do not know about.

Conflict – Are your team meetings full of energy and lively debate?

Do exchanges take place that are heated or are they polite? Or are your team meetings quiet as people are afraid of speaking out?

Conflict is healthy and desirable when it is constructive. When trust exists in teams, members are more willing to speak out, to disagree, to risk their opinion being heard. There is less likelihood of people talking negatively about one another behind their backs. Help your team to develop positive approaches to conflict. See The Mindful Approach to Conflict Page 33 for more information. In your team meetings when you notice negative behaviours taking place, what do you do? Do you ignore the eyes rolling? The silent disagreement? Are people distracted by their phones or tablets? Do you challenge these behaviours? If not, why not? What behaviours are you silently consenting to?

Commitment – How committed are your team to the actions and objectives that they are set?

The team is committed when it moves forward without hesitation; when it shows innovative approaches and is able to change fluidly with new initiatives. Discussions are not revisited over and over again, people are not afraid of trying new things and learning from their mistakes. How do you get commitment? It comes from clarity and buy in. Clarity from communication and buy in from the building of trust and inviting dialogue and debate. What is the vision? Do you have one? How has it been shared with the team? Have the team been involved in shaping it? How will the vision be achieved? What are the objectives that have been set and how have the team contributed? It's easier to commit when you are involved shaping the pathway to the end goal.

Accountability – Do team members hold one another to account?

Is poor performance addressed and not tolerated by the team? Are problems dealt with quickly and potential problems identified?

Ambiguity is the enemy of accountability. If people do not know what is expected of them then how can they be accountable? To achieve accountability, all the other steps need to be in place first. The environment needs to be created in which people will feel discomfort if they are not accountable. Goals and objectives need to be agreed and published and discussed regularly and feedback given. It's not just the leader's responsibility to hold everyone accountable - it is for each team member to hold themselves accountable and to notice and act when any team member is not delivering.

Results – Are the team motivated by collective results or on personal success?

Is individual status or team status more important in achieving results? Perhaps an opportunity to downsize/upsize is not welcomed even though doing so would mean greater success? How is success rewarded? Is it based on individual or team performance or a mixture of both?

These steps for high performing teams come from Patrick Lencioni in his book *The Five Dysfunctions of a Team*. Being mindful of each of these steps will change the team dynamic. Being mindful means being aware of what is actually happening within the team and knowing what needs to change. Making the changes effortlessly by not judging the behaviours, instead by raising everyone's awareness about what is happening, what is going on.

By helping each member of the team to become more aware, more understanding of one another's needs, more open and honest and more team-focused, the team is likely to flourish. If team members work together through the above questions and use it as a team development opportunity, the result will be a more mindful, more aware and more focused team.

Summary
- **Notice your inner dialogue. What thoughts do you need to change?**
- **Identify how you can build trust in the team**
- **Encourage healthy conflict**
- **Ensure that clarity can lead to commitment**
- **Help team members to hold one another accountable**
- **Develop conditions for team success**

The Mindful Approach to

Managing time

It is true to say that we all have the same amount of time available to us and yet it can feel like it's never enough. Sometimes the expectations of speed of response, the number of people we are connected to and the potential for being connected 24/7 mean that we can feel overwhelmed and unable to stay on top of our workload. A mindful approach to time management makes it possible to feel in control and can enhance your productivity.

Making lists

Making lists of all of the tasks that need to be completed is the starting point for a lot of people. A list is a good thing; it helps you to see how many tasks you need to address. Lists are good for getting clarity and for taking all of that information out of your head so that you can let go of the less critical tasks and create some space in your mind to concentrate on the more important ones.

A downside of lists is that we normally do a brain dump onto paper of all of those tasks that we have on our mind without prioritising them. We write those tasks down in the order that they pop into our minds. Time management is about deciding on those tasks that will support your success and how much time you will spend on them. As you complete your list, survey it mindfully and notice your internal response. What thoughts do you have about your work? Notice the feelings the list creates and any physical response. Be curious and bring this awareness to the next stage: goal setting.

Setting a goal

The first step in time management is to be clear on what your goal is. Is it enhancing performance of the team? Achieving the sales targets? Launching a new product or project? What is most important for you to achieve your overall goals? Once you have clarity on that then you can begin to focus your time and energy. If everything appears to be urgent and important, it's time for a mindful pause. If you had to justify how you'd chosen what you're working on to your boss, what would you choose to focus on?

Without a goal for the day, or the week, or your role, it is easy to get lost in distractions that happen: the constant stream of emails that arrive in your inbox, the instant messages that pop up, enticing you away from the task in hand, offers of the day, text messages, requests for help from colleagues, phone calls etc.

Prioritise

In *The Seven Habits of Highly Effective People* by Stephen R. Covey there is a very good analogy that will help you to understand why prioritisation is important. The story from the book suggests that you define your work in the following three ways:

- Rocks -those tasks that are critical to your and/or your team's success. They align to your objectives. 80% of your success will be attributable to these vital few tasks which represent 20% of the things in your to do list. There may be 4 or 5 of these.
- Pebbles - these tasks are not as important as the rocks but need to be addressed; if not they may cause problems further down the line. These might be telephone calls from customers, paper work that needs doing, meetings, some projects, some emails.
- Sand - the things that come in on a daily and frequent basis that are not very important but need to be done. They may be administrative tasks, phone calls, the odd request.

Now imagine that your day is a big glass jar and that the tasks that you are going to fill your day up with are labelled Rocks, Pebbles and Sand.

If you focus on filling your jar with tasks labelled as sand and pebbles first, then there will not be enough space to fill in the remainder of the jar with rocks. Your time will be spent doing interesting web searches, reading and answering non urgent emails as they come in. These are the tasks that need doing but do not take priority on the project that you are working on. The rocks i.e. the tasks that align with your objectives and define your success should always be allocated space in your jar/time in your day first.

If the rocks are put in the jar first then there will be room for some of the pebble tasks – emails, research, phone calls and may even have room for a little sand – social conversations, networking, non-urgent emails etc. Deal with the rocks first. A more mindful awareness and understanding of which tasks are rocks, pebbles and sand will lead to more mindful choices about how you spend your time.

Beware of auto pilot

When a friend of ours changed jobs, she told us that in the first few weeks she had driven to her old office a few times! This is an example of being on autopilot where we have programmed our minds to react without conscious thought or effort. Being on autopilot is an important capability for some things in life, for example, not having to think about how to eat, brush your teeth, get dressed, etc. but time may not be used most efficiently when you operate on autopilot in the workplace.

A good example is reading your emails that keep on popping up but have nothing to do with your most important objective of the day. Another example is saying 'yes' to a request that is not part of your role or function but you just say you will do it to help a colleague out or because it feels awkward saying no. Your autopilot may lead to you working on tasks that are aligned to your pebbles or sand, not your rocks and they soon eat up your time leaving you with less time to focus on the rocks. Alternatively, you may find your work hours increasing as your day has been hijacked by the pebbles and you still need to get to those rocks!

Mindful steps

Be aware of where you are spending your time – log every activity that you do for a week on your calendar. Ask yourself how much time do you spend reading emails? How often do you check your phone? How much time do you spend in meetings? Do you have to be in those meetings?

Identify those vital few tasks, that critical 20% of tasks that will drive your success and spend 80% of your time doing these things. What are those one or two things, that when you do them well, deliver great results? These are your rocks.

Pay attention in the moment to that job you are doing. When working on a piece of work, is your mind on that email that just popped up? These mini distractions break concentration and slow down progress and thought processes. Switch off the pop up email box and notice how that makes a difference to your day.

Have a goal for how you will spend the extra time saved by using these techniques. If you could improve your effectiveness by 10% a day, that is approximately 48 minutes a day for an 8 hour shift, how would you spend that 'extra' time? Set yourself a goal. Perhaps it would be possible to take a nice lunch break; network with colleagues; go for a walk; leave a little earlier; do more research.

Time stealers

Some of the reasons you may feel you don't have enough time could be linked to your definition of success. If, for example, success is defined by working the longest hours, responding to emails late at night, saying 'yes' to most of the requests that come your way; attending meetings that you don't add value to; confusing being busy and being productive; thinking that doing more means that you are inexpendable - then 24 hours in a day may never be enough.

Before saying 'yes' to a request from a colleague, manager or customer, ask:

Is this task aligned to my goal?

Will saying 'yes!' tip the balance for me?

Can I say 'no', suggest a colleague deals with it, or delegate it as a development opportunity for someone else?

Distractions

Mindfulness is about paying attention and having greater clarity and focus in the moment. If you do not make a conscious choice of how to spend your time wisely, then you are unlikely to be efficient or effective in your work, and may choose to work instead on whatever is top of your mind or what you feel most like doing at that time. These distractions can lead to tasks taking more time than if you were working in a focused and undistracted way. Focused attention creates more opportunity for freeing up pockets of time.

Summary

- **Be present, focused, in the moment. Pay attention to the task you are involved in – notice how much easier it is to complete**
- **Know what defines your 'rocks' and do those tasks that align to them first**
- **Beware of time stealers and say 'no' more**
- **Minimise distractions**
- **Don't confuse being busy with being productive**

The Mindful Approach to

Emails

How mindful are you when sending, receiving and managing emails? Emails are an efficient, fast and easy way of communicating. These positives can have a downside; the volume of emails can lead to a mind-set of fast, efficient response which means they can sometimes lack the finesse of a face to face conversation. This applies whether you are the sender, the receiver or trying to get/stay on top of your inbox. A mindful approach to emailing can yield benefits in terms of relationships and results, as bringing more conscious awareness to sending and receiving emails will improve the quality of your written communication and may even reduce the amount of email traffic if messages are clearer in their intent.

Emails are sent and received with incomplete information

When we talk to another person face to face we use a code that involves words, dance and music. The words are what we choose to say. The dance is the body language used to express ourselves and the music is the tone of voice - the pauses, emphasis and emotion in the voice.

Lots of this richness and tone of voice is stripped away when communicating via emails and that means that the meaning of the message can be lost and/or misinterpreted, resulting in a different impact from that originally intended.

Receiving emails

Opening up an email can provoke an emotional response. Maybe it signals more work; hard to answer questions; a reschedule of a plan; bad news; request for urgent information; an opportunity; an invitation…. It can be all too easy to choose a fast, ill thought through response rather than a mindful one.

Writing and reading emails in a mindful way may help you to respond appropriately and professionally, minimising regrets and relationship damage.

When you receive an email and it evokes an emotional response, read it carefully several times. Now take three mindful breaths to still the mind.

Notice what feelings are present at this moment? Notice what thoughts you are having? Do not get caught up in the thoughts, simply notice them and bring your attention back to your breath for three more breaths. Read the email again with a still mind.

Sending emails

Is your mind still and ready to write the email with the right emotional approach or is some more time needed to gain clarity and be present in the moment?

Before you decide to reply to a potentially difficult email, pause, breathe and imagine the recipient. Take time to visualise the person that the email is intended for. Picture them in your mind; imagine you see the situation from their viewpoint. Be curious about what prompted them to write the email? What might be their intention? What might they be trying to achieve? Imagine them receiving your email. What impact might it have? Is it the impact that you want?

Think about what you want to convey. If you are planning a hurried response because you are short of time, check that this is appropriate for the message and for the person you're sending it too. It's easy to pride yourself on multi-tasking whilst emailing and being efficient when in reality it means insufficient attention is being paid to the emailing and whatever else you are doing at the time.

As you write, ensure you are giving a clear message and that you consider how that message will be received. Your words and your style of writing can compensate somewhat for the lack of visual and verbal clues in your communication. Stay connected to your own thoughts and feelings as you write to the receiver(s) as people who also have thoughts and feelings.

Once you have finished writing take a few breaths and read the email. Re-read it to make sure that your message will be received with the intention that you meant and that it will be understood.

Once satisfied, press send.

Managing your email workload

The number of emails in your inbox can weigh heavily on your mind. Those in bold that have yet to be opened can be tempting. Those that have been opened and require a response, which you have yet to write can feel like unfinished business. Then there are those that you need to read, which you keep for when you've got time. But you never have time. Managing the flow of emails so that they do not dominate your working life can be challenging and we can be lured into dealing with them on auto pilot. It can be easy to open up emails as soon as they arrive, just out of curiosity, which you then return to later. Even if you deal with them in the moment, you may have stopped doing something that could be more important. This is both distracting and inefficient.

A technique for email efficiency

How efficient is it to keep checking your phone/tablet/laptop intermittently throughout the day, reading and re-reading emails, building up in our heads all the things that need to be done?

A more mindful approach for managing emails is to check and respond when we can get ourselves in the right state to do so, calmly, rationally and efficiently as described above. What if you checked your email at certain intervals for a certain length of time? e.g. for 30 minutes, at the start, middle and end of the day.

Notice what thoughts and feelings you have about this suggestion. Email checking can be like an addiction. Commit to become more aware of how many times a day you get the urge to check email. Notice what thoughts and feelings arise if you choose not to be led by that thought.

Choosing to be more mindful about email checking and responding can lead to better focus and more productivity all round: Better quality email interactions and better quality other work as you retain focus on what's most important in your work, without constant distraction. Let it be known when you access your emails so that people's expectations can be managed and they can choose alternative means of contacting you in times when an urgent response is needed.

What is the best way of dealing with those emails that you are Cc'd into or Bcc'd? Consider setting up a separate folder for these and let people know that if a response is needed from you then it's better to include you on the email cascade in the To: line. Adopt this practice in your own sending of emails too.

Consider other ways of communicating. If your message is urgent, perhaps setting up a face to face meeting is more appropriate, or a telephone call. Emails are an effective mode of communication but they are one of many. Being mindful of your use of emails can enhance your impact so it pays to pause and be mindful of whether what you need to say is best said in an email or not. Taking control of emails in a mindful way allows you to control your work proactively rather than reacting to whatever is in front of you.

Summary

- **Read your emails with a still mind by focusing on your breath before responding**
- **Re-read your response; still your mind; read it again before sending**
- **Manage your approach to emails, choose when you will open your inbox**
- **Remember emails are only one mode of communication. Ask yourself if an email is the best response for your message.**

The Mindful Approach to

Meetings

Do you sometimes feel that your day is spent sitting in or rushing from meeting to meeting? It has been reported that two thirds of meetings end before an important decision is made. How many meetings have you left feeling dissatisfied because the meeting has failed to achieve its goal? In this chapter we explore how taking a mindful approach can change your experience of meetings and enhance their effectiveness.

We will look at using mindfulness in meetings that you have been invited to attend so that you can pay full attention and add maximum value. We will also look at how you can chair your own meetings and get maximum buy in from all attending.

Meeting invitations

Imagine you have just received an email invitation to attend a meeting that is connected to the project that you are part of. Taking a mindful approach to attending meetings starts with pausing before you accept the invitation; take three long, slow, mindful breaths to clear space for clarity of thought. Now with your total attention on the subject of whether you attend this meeting ask yourself three questions:

- What is the purpose of my attendance?
- Am I needed in that meeting or can one of my team attend in my place?
- What can I do to add value?

Most managers that we talk to have a diary filled with back to back meetings that they attend because someone has invited them. It can be easy to accept meeting invitations with only a brief, 'I suppose I should/ought to..' and without thinking that by saying 'yes' to the meeting, that it means saying 'no' to something else. When pressed many admit that actually they probably do not need to be present at many of those meetings, as the purpose of the meeting was an update or information cascade and perhaps they could have sent someone else or that information could have been communicated in an email. Meetings are the most expensive means of sharing information. Think about the cost of you sitting in a meeting for 45 minutes, not adding or receiving value and multiply that by the number of people in the room! Being mindful about whether you attend or not may just save costs on the bottom line.

Preparing for the meeting

You have decided to attend the meeting and you have accepted the meeting invitation. Before you go to the meeting take time to prepare mindfully. Take time to do ten breaths or the three step breathing space. You can find guides for these practices in the Appendix on Page 117. Turn your attention to your purpose of attending the meeting. Maybe it's to hear the latest updates, to network, build credibility, ask questions, share information, add value, or even for political reasons? Whatever your purpose is for attending, be clear on this. Create a picture in your mind of how you want to act – confident; curious; the expert; devil's advocate; team player? How do you want to feel emotionally? Calm and collected? Frustrated? Annoyed? Enthusiastic? What are the two or three key points that you might want to make?

Being in the meeting

It is possible to be in one meeting physically and in another mentally. When you attend the meeting that you have already decided is worthwhile attending, you need to make sure that you are in the meeting, totally present and paying attention in the moment. Just before you leave your desk or on the journey to the meeting or at the very latest just as you enter the meeting, check that in your mind you are not still processing the last meeting that you attended; or that you are not going over the paper work that you left on your desk or the conversation that you just had with a colleague on the way into the meeting. Check also that your mind is not preparing for the next meeting after this one or preparing for writing that report; worrying about how long the meeting will last or a myriad of other concerns. Use the three step breathing space (see Appendix Page 118) to be aware of your thoughts and feelings, turn your attention to your breath for a few breaths and then expand your awareness to how you are now in this moment, bringing your attention to being there in the meeting room.

Chairing a meeting

You have reached a decision that you need to call a meeting. Prior to sending out the meeting invitations, you have taken the mindful approach and asked yourself, 'Is the meeting really necessary?' 'What are the outcomes that I want to achieve?' 'Who needs to be at that meeting and what value will they bring?'

Being mindful in organising the meeting will ensure that you have the right people there, all of whom are clear on their contribution value and clear on the purpose of the meeting. In short, the meeting will be focused and effectiveness will be enhanced.

Managing internal dialogue

All meetings chaired with a mindful approach are important events, otherwise you would not be holding them. You have not accessed your auto pilot in calling for the meeting, instead you have a clear objective in getting this group of people together. Next you want to ensure that the outcome is achieved. Our emotional state is driven by the thoughts that we are having - our internal dialogue. The way that we act out these feelings will determine how effective we are, our results and our behaviours. Perhaps the internal dialogue is around the need to be right and to prove the other parties in the meeting wrong. This will create a feeling of tension and possible conflict and it will also close your mind down to seeking creative solutions and mutual problem solving.

Perhaps your internal dialogue is around your emotions, being careful not to show what you are really feeling, how frustrated you are about the progress made or people's attitudes. A word of caution... feelings usually leak out and people can read how we are feeling through our body language and tone of voice. The mindful approach is to take some time before starting the meeting to check in with yourself and ask 'How am I feeling?' 'How do I want to show up at the meeting?' 'Am I in the optimum emotional state to be effective in the meeting and if not what can I do about it?'

Chances are if you are feeling any negative emotions, they are the result of something that has taken place before this moment or they are the result of a picture that you are constructing in your mind about something that has not yet happened, and might never happen! So let go of that thought as thoughts are not actual events they are re runs of past events or pre plays of future events and not always helpful.

Check your body language. The way you stand or sit affects your feelings and your behaviours. How you behave will influence your impact during the meeting and the outcome that you want.

Start the meeting

Now you are ready to start the meeting. The first thing to pay attention to is what is happening in the room? Are people chatting and catching up with each other? Is the atmosphere light and relaxed or is it tense? Are there dynamics within the room that you need to be aware of? You can help people to fully arrive in the meeting, by inviting them to take a few minutes to be focused on this meeting. Simply thank them for attending; acknowledge that you know they are busy people and ask them to commit to being fully present in this meeting for the next thirty minutes (or however long the meeting lasts). Ask if there is anything that will prevent them from being fully present, and if there is, allow them the option of dealing with it.

Some companies have started to begin their meetings by inviting everyone to take three breaths to bring themselves right here, right now so that they are not distracted by planning, worrying, thinking about the next meeting and other factors apart from why they are in this meeting.

Running the meeting

Next, state the intention of the meeting so that everyone is mindful why you are all together. Invite everyone to stay fully present at the meeting and potentially spend a couple of minutes agreeing what this means in practice. This could be things like mobiles off, fully listening, allowing everyone space to think and ask questions etc.

Guide the various stages of the meeting, this may include: –

- Stating the problem
- Sharing the agenda
- Generating and evaluating ideas
- Making a decision
- Planning next steps

Keep to time, avoid 'meeting creep' when the meeting starts late because of stragglers turning up late and then ends late. You can avoid this by sticking to the agenda and keeping control. Be known for chairing meetings that have a purpose, start on time and finish on time. When, or if, conflicts and disagreements arise, invite the group to take three breaths together. In doing this you are helping the meeting to re-focus, be present and disengage from ruminations and unhelpful energy.

Check in with yourself during the meeting and make sure that you are present and not somewhere else in your mind. Use your breath as an anchor to bring you back to the present moment if for any reason you find yourself lost in thought about a comment or emotionally reacting. People will perceive your pausing as being a moment to reflect, used wisely this can add to your gravitas and will defuse conflict moments.

Just before you close the meeting make sure that everyone has the opportunity to contribute their thoughts. Ask 'Are there any other comments?' Go round everyone individually so that they feel valued and heard. It may be that you cannot deal with their comment in this meeting and that you will need to pick the comment up with them later on or table for discussion in the next meeting. It can also be useful to review the effectiveness of the meeting in terms of objectives achieved, behaviours and process. Every meeting is an opportunity to learn how to be more effective next time.

Summary
- **Take time to prepare mentally and physically before the meeting using the breath**
- **Be clear on your purpose**
- **Manage your inner dialogue during the meeting**
- **Use mindfulness to keep the meeting focused and on track by taking time to reset**

The Mindful Approach to

Technology

The amount of information available to us is both amazing and overwhelming; it gives us tremendous advantages and value when used appropriately. For many of us it is difficult to unplug from the stream of information around us and we can become slaves to technology. Wherever you are, just pause for a moment. Look up from this page and look around you. If you are in a busy office, or in a café, how many people can you see on a mobile or a tablet device? Reading a book, magazine? Is there a television on or radio? Music playing in the background? All of these things can distract us and pull us away from the present moment.

The good and bad of social media

It is important that you are aware of how much time you spend not fully 'in the moment'.

It is a curious phenomenon when technology that is meant to help us to connect to one another loses its true purpose and becomes a means of disconnection. How many times do you see people in meetings, with colleagues, eating lunch, not focusing on the people they are with, but studying their phones and tablets; checking that they are not missing the latest news or a message from someone? What might that imply about the importance of the people who are physically there with them? What damage might this do to relationships over time?

Plugged in 24/7?

Constantly checking phones for messages, updates, emails, news and calls can become a habit that we unconsciously adopt and one which can become addictive. This can take its toll on us, adding to a sense of overwhelm and stress. The fear of not knowing what's going on can drive these behaviours in us and threaten our inner peace and connection to what's going on in the present.

Social media

Social media was originally developed as a means of connecting people together. It's ironic that at times it may do the opposite, encouraging people to connect via media rather than fully connect in person. Social media can create self-doubt; all of those messages and comments that you need to reply to, the guilt about not having posted as frequently as you 'should'; concerns about whether you have enough followers or whether your pictures and posts are as interesting and dynamic as other people's. What did they mean by that comment? How should I respond? Consider taking a more mindful approach to social media which means that you are selective about what you access and when you access it. Take a mindful pause and consider the following questions before you reach for your device:

- Is telling people what you are doing right now more important than doing it?
- What difference will it make if you look at your emails now or later when you have scheduled time for working?
- What are you missing right here and right now when you are distracted by the noise of social media?
- When you post that comment is it a comment that you would happily tell someone face to face?
- How do the people/person that you are with feel about your view that something else is more important than being totally present with them?

How is social media impacting you?

To analyse the extent of the impact that social media is having on you ask yourself these questions:

Are you feeling guilty for not posting enough?

Do you feel pressurised to post more often?

What is your purpose for using social media? Is it to create a presence about your brand, hobby? Is it to share ideas? Is it to stay connected with friends and family? Is it for inspiration or friendship?

Why do you follow the people that you follow? Do you automatically follow people because they follow you? Do you have an interest in certain subjects? If people are uninteresting do you unfollow them?

Do your activities on social media align with your purpose for using social media? Do all social media channels address your needs?

Asking yourself these questions brings mindfulness into play and enables you to make choices and take actions consciously. When you are fully present in the actions that you are taking then you are in control and more able to make decisions that are enabling rather than detracting you from that which is important right here and right now, moment by moment.

Text messages and instant messages

Texting and instant messaging can be a quick and easy way of communicating. The downside is that they can create a culture in which we feel compelled to respond immediately. The subtleties of communication, like body language, facial expressions, gesticulations, tone of voice are all absent in text messages and instant messaging, this means that you are reliant only on the content of the message.

Use text messages and instant messaging mindfully. Slow down and read the message; take a few mindful breaths; re-read the message; write your reply; take three breaths; re-read; send the message. If the reply is not understood, pick up the phone and speak to the person rather than getting lost in a long chain of text messages.

Summary

- **Stop, pause, breathe and decide if now is the right time to engage with technology**
- **Be conscious of how your use of technology impacts the people you are with**
- **Notice how technology can take you away from the present moment and decide if that is what you want**

The Mindful Approach to

Presentation anxiety

Presentations are often an unavoidable part of working life yet many people are terrified of standing up and talking in front of groups whether large or small. A mindful approach can help you to manage those nerves so that your focus is on the group and the impact you're making rather than your own discomfort. Let's face it, it's hard to be confident if your mind is busy with thoughts of:

What if ... I lose track of where I am/forget stuff/make a fool of myself/embarrass myself/clam up?

What if ... people look bored/someone asks me a question I can't answer/someone laughs at me/gets angry?

Any such internal worries undermine your ability to be really mindful, to be really present and therefore undermine your ability to be responsive to the audience and be at your best.

Before the presentation

Planning

Presenting mindfully starts at the point of planning your presentation.

Before you write a word or design a slide, think about the purpose of your presentation. Sit quietly for a few moments and bring your attention to your breath; follow the path of your breath into and out of your body for a count of ten breaths; gently bring your attention to the presentation and ask yourself what is the purpose of this presentation?

Now imagine your audience. Breathe deeply and imagine them in the room. How much do they know about the subject? What might capture their interest? Now think from your perspective about what you need the audience to Know, Believe and Do at the end of this presentation.

Know - what knowledge do you want them to have gained?

Believe - what do you want them to feel/trust is true?

Do - what action do you want them to take as a result of this presentation?

Having considered what's important to the audience and the purpose of your presentation, you are now ready to design your presentation. As you do so, check regularly that it's meeting the audience's needs and achieving what you set out to do. As you are writing, imagine yourself delivering it; what is the right style? Do you want to energise the audience? Have an interactive session? Or something else?

Practice

Poise and confidence when presenting comes from being comfortable with your material and being prepared for the questions that might be asked. Practice out loud, not just the content of what you are planning to say but also practice using your voice and body language to create an effective and engaging presentation. Think about the kind of questions that might be asked and think about how you would handle any questions you don't know the answer to. If possible, practice in front of someone who is prepared to give you honest feedback. Ask them to point out three things that you did well for every one thing they advise you to change. This ensures the feedback is designed to build your self-confidence and also gives them permission to suggest something you can improve on.

Just before the presentation and as the presentation begins

To enable you to feel calm as you stand up to present, take some deep breaths and relax your entire body, noticing any thoughts that come up in your head and taking care not to get caught up in your thinking. You are not your thoughts. Be aware of your feet planted firmly on the floor and feel the support of the ground; feel grounded.

During the presentation

Gary Genard, in his book, *Fearless Speaking* defines mindfulness in this context as 'the ability to speak to audiences with total awareness of the task and the people at hand'.

So you are aware of what you are saying and you are tuned into the audience and how they are responding. Your point of focus needs to be the audience and meeting their needs rather than concern for your own performance. Any internal questioning, wondering or self-criticism takes you away from being 'present' and being wrapped up in self- judgement. As inner thoughts do come up, take a moment to acknowledge and refocus on the audience.

Use all your senses when presenting: Connect to the audience through eye contact. Use your voice as a tool to engage them by varying its tone, pitch and speed. Use emphasis to make a point. Allow your body to relax and use hand gestures naturally to enhance your speech. Slow everything down and really feel your words coming to life. Use pauses to create impact.

Carmine Gallo in *The Presentation Secrets of Steve Jobs* says, 'Nothing is more dramatic than a well-placed pause… Jobs does not rush his presentation. He lets it breathe. He will often remain quiet for a few seconds as he lets a key point sink in'.

Dealing with those wobbly moments

If you have a wobbly moment during a presentation, for example someone challenges you or asks a question to which you have no instant answer, stop and take a deep breath.

Pause and notice your thoughts, feelings and body sensations. Noticing helps you to retain some distance and objectivity without getting caught up in unhelpful thoughts or disruptive feelings or unpleasant sensations. You can disguise this by appearing to be deep in thought or by taking a sip of water.

Once you've stopped and taken a breath, think. Slow down your thinking so you're able to focus on getting back on track and make an appropriate response.

Re-focus on the purpose of your presentation and what the audience needs.

An alternative strategy is to move; just a few steps to release the tension or alternatively, focus your attention on feeling your feet on the ground. As you feel more grounded, take a deep breath and make a conscious decision to relax the body. Release any tension that's accumulating in the face, shoulders or legs. Be in your body, not in your head.

The important thing is to stay connected to your audience.

The more that's going on inside your own head, the less you will be connecting with the audience.

Notice your internal dialogue and listen for self-judgement; if you're judging your performance, you're not presenting mindfully. If you notice with awareness your internal dialogue and simply label it 'judging', you're not getting caught up in it and can move your focus to where it needs to be to the content, delivery and the audience.

After the presentation

It's now time to relax and reflect on your experience. Take the opportunity to tune into your own thoughts and feelings about how the presentation has gone and seek out feedback from the audience on their perspective.

Ask specifically for feedback on what went well and what you should think about doing differently next time.

Capture the feedback and your own thoughts and feelings as your learning from this presentation will enable you to present more confidently and more mindfully next time.

Summary

- **What do your audience need to know, believe and do at the end of the presentation?**
- **Rehearse your presentation**
- **Breathe consciously**
- **Be aware of your thinking and avoid getting caught up in these thoughts**
- **Focus on meeting the audience's needs**
- **Pause, breathe and focus on the audience if you are unsettled**

The Mindful Approach to

Leadership

A mindful leader has the ability to make moment to moment decisions, based on a careful assessment of relevant data, combined with the clarity of thinking to recognise the impact of this decision making. A leader lacking in mindfulness is more likely to react in a habitual or instinctive way with less attention paid to the consequences.

On auto pilot

We have built routines into our lives, to reduce the number of choices we have to make each day e.g same seat on the train, car parking space, lunch etc. This can be helpful in preventing decision fatigue when it's about low risk decisions; it becomes more problematic if we frequently act out of conscious awareness in conversations, meetings, or in deciding how we use our time; what gets our attention and what doesn't.

What if being busy at work encourages you to behave as if you are on auto-pilot? What if you have a habitual way of reacting? How aware are you of the impact of your reaction on others? What if you spend most of the day with your attention only partly on what you are doing? You might be talking to a team member but thinking about a report you have to complete before the end of the day. Or on a conference call but glancing over your emails. Mindfulness can help you focus your attention. It can help reconnect with what is actually going on and what is truly important. It can help improve the quality of your work and your relationships.

Take time for yourself

In order to lead others effectively, it's important to feel in a good place yourself to do so. Taking time for yourself to practice mindfulness whilst sitting helps you think more clearly, engage more fully and manage your energy. It gives you time to tune into what you are thinking, notice how you are feeling, and to develop improved awareness of what's going on for those around you. Relationships improve, communication is clearer and understanding grows. Being a better leader starts with self-awareness and awareness of how you impact other people; mindful sitting can support your growth in self-awareness.

Self-reflection

Taking time to reflect on your performance and impact as a leader, maybe journaling about this, maybe talking it through with a coach, will build your self-awareness further. Reflecting on what's gone well, what could have gone better and committing to making conscious changes will further enhance your leadership ability. Self-reflection is always enhanced and balanced by seeking feedback from others on how you can be a better leader.

Overcoming obstacles

We have noticed when working with leaders, the extent to which they get in their own way! Three ways in which this plays out are:

- **Inner dialogue** – we all talk constantly to ourselves, in our heads. Go ahead and listen in for a moment. What thoughts are you having right now? You may surprise yourself as to the balance of positive thoughts to negative thoughts. Tune in for a while today and notice how often you say 'I'm really proud of that' or, ' that was a good response I gave to that question' versus how many times you think, 'why did I say that in that way?' 'I wish I had…..' 'I'm not good at this.' We limit ourselves with our own inner dialogues about what we believe we can or can't do.

  Our inner dialogue is based on our interpretation of a past experience, something that we did that perhaps did not work very well. We tend to hang onto that thought and the feeling that it creates long after the event. We keep it in some easily accessible recess of our mind so that we can pull it out as a memory just when we are faced with a similar situation again. Be aware of your inner dialogue. Notice what your inner voice is saying and notice how it impacts you.

- **Worry** - the narrative here is about something that could happen in the future. 'What if I make the wrong decision?' 'What's going to happen if…?' It's easy to get in a discussion with ourselves about a future that hasn't happened yet. If we have these concerns for the future and set about planning how to ensure our fears are not realised, this can be helpful. We go into conscious planning mode as opposed to unconscious rumination mode.

- If we're simply thinking about future negative possibilities, we put our brains on alert to a perceived danger that doesn't really exist, apart from in our heads! But just like a real threat to our life we will produce the same hormones that will help us to fight, flight or freeze when exposed to danger. The difference is when the danger is in real life (e.g. a potentially challenging meeting), we stop producing the hormones once the danger has passed, but when we worry about a perceived danger, our brains treat it as still being present and will continue to produce the stress hormones. It is this response that creates stress in our bodies and may potentially lead to illness. The stress will lead to a reduction in the capability of performing at our best with clarity of mind and focus. Be aware of your thinking patterns; label any anxious thoughts, 'here's worry' and let the thoughts move away.

- **Busyness** - we can find ourselves so busy just 'doing' – in the detail, getting bogged down by working **in** the job rather than **on** the job. We miss the big picture because we are overwhelmed by the minutiae of the present. We attend meetings because we 'have' to be there (or even worse 'have to be seen to be there'); we involve ourselves in tasks that ideally someone else should be doing, perhaps because of the volume of work that needs to be done by the ever shortening deadline. Or maybe it's because there hasn't been time to upskill the capability of the team so 'I'm the only one who can do this / I don't trust anyone else'

If you're the kind of person who answers, 'I'm busy' to the question, 'How are you?' then recognise the busyness, and identify what's driving the busyness. Know that it's OK to press the pause button, breathe and just notice your thoughts.

What's your narrative?

Becoming more mindful as a leader is about noticing the story you are telling yourself, noticing the narrative running through your mind.

The second step is to change the narrative if necessary. What is your inner voice saying and to what extent does it support you as a mindful leader?

Meditation

As you read this, stop and take ten seconds to focus on your breathing and ask yourself 'Am I the leader I want to be?'

Build an image in your mind of the type of leader you want to be. What values do you hold? How do you demonstrate these values in your day to day work? How do you make your decisions? How do you communicate? What impact do you have on people? What are people saying about you? What is your reputation?

As this image builds in your mind, notice how it makes you feel. Focus on that feeling, without changing it in any way. Complete the following statement.

The leader that I am is: ....

Forming connections

Leadership is about relationships and your ability to engage with others. If you tend to be thinking about the past, re-running old scenarios or tend to be thinking ahead about the future, it may be that you miss something that's going on in the present. If you immerse yourself in the detail without standing back to see the big picture, you could miss some of the people impact. When you speak to people, are you clear on what you want to achieve? You inspire others when you stay connected to what is important, when you are clear on what it is you care about. Mindful leaders have a heightened sense of self-awareness and awareness of what's important to others.

Find alignment

What kind of future are you working towards? What is guiding you? Be clear about the outcomes that you want in the future. Make sure that the way you think, behave, communicate and connect with others are aligned to your beliefs, values and vision. As a mindful leader, you are conscious of these things and are guided by your desired future direction every day.

Be at your best, more of the time.

How can you be at your best more of the time? Your behaviour affects the behaviour of everyone around you. People around you are watching you: You are always on show, in the office, at lunch, in your car, socially. Be aware of this; be mindful of this. Check in with yourself as you pause and breathe, 'How am I being in this moment? Am I being the leader I want to be?'

Some leaders meditate daily, sometimes more than once and some take mindful pauses throughout the day to enter into a more mindful state. One leader described his practice of meditating as a time to still his mind, to quiet the noise and be with what is present, to be able to think clearly. The ability to be self-aware of what is here, now, with no judgement, just noticing, is at the heart of being a mindful and effective leader. Mindfulness is one way in which you can gift yourself the time to be present, to get to know yourself better and be able to be more choiceful in what you say and do.

Practicing mindful breathing for ten to twenty minutes a day can help you to develop into a more authentic leader who is more fully present in relationships and getting the job done.

Summary

- **To be effective as a leader it is important to pay attention, be in the moment**
- **Take time to reflect on the kind of leader you want to be**
- **Focus on the breath to train the mind to retain focus on the things that really matter**
- **Use mindfulness as a way of managing your internal dialogue and forging better relationships**

The Mindful Approach to
Coaching

Your ability to coach your team members is an important part of your role as a manager. Coaching is an essential skill to help your team members and other colleagues develop, learn and grow in their roles. It encourages them to work things out for themselves, to think things through. Coaching mindfully takes your skills to another level. It's about being self-aware as you talk; it's about being highly aware of the other person and acutely observing their behaviours and body language and listening to all different aspects of their voice as well as noting their choice of words. It's about noticing your own thoughts, feelings and physical sensations and choosing not to be distracted by the information you're picking up. Mindful coaching will make you a better coach. This means making a better job of developing your team members and bringing about positive changes in them.

Coaching can take place at any time either formally when you have one to one time set aside or informally if you are approached with a problem, an opportunity or if someone is stuck in some way.

How does coaching help?

When you coach, you're inviting the person being coached to:

- Become more self-aware
- Take time to reflect on thinking, feelings and behaviours
- Challenge unhelpful ways of thinking
- Become aware of what's really important
- Make changes/develop/learn/grow
- Set goals and see new possibilities
- Identify new ways of thinking and behaving
- Become more resourceful and self-reliant
- Build resilience
- Increase effectiveness at work

In order to encourage these outcomes, it's clear how important it is for the person coaching to be:

- Fully present
- Fully aware with focused attention
- Able to manage emotions effectively
- Non-judgemental

All of the above are developed through mindfulness. Arguably, it's simply not possible to coach in a truly effective way without a mindful approach.

Before you have a coaching conversation

If you have a coaching session with a team member, take a short while to prepare beforehand. As well as taking time to think through the content of what you want to say and work on. Take a few moments to prepare yourself with a few deep breaths and the intention to bring yourself to the present moment with awareness and attention. It's easy to rush into one of these kinds of meetings at the last minute, thinking about something that's just happened, or thinking about something you need to do later. If you don't bring your full awareness and attention to the interaction, you will be less effective as a coach and as a manager. Taking a three step breathing space may also benefit you here. See Appendix on Page 118 for a guide on the process.

Engaging a mindful coaching approach in the moment

If someone approaches you with a problem/query/opportunity, take the opportunity to use a coaching approach to expand their thinking. Choose not to offer your opinion, instead, hold the intention to create the space for them to explore their situation fully. You may not have the opportunity to take a few deep breaths or take a breathing space before you reply, so instead, consciously take a breath and pause, before responding. Bring awareness in the moment to your own body, sitting or standing. Notice how your body feels, are there any areas of tension? How are you feeling emotionally? Then bring your awareness to the person speaking to you. What do you notice about their body language? What do you notice about how they are speaking; the volume/tone/pace of their voice? This attention to yourself and the other person only takes a few seconds in total but brings you to the present moment, with awareness.

During the coaching conversation

- Focus on the other person, listen to them fully, notice how they appear
- Ask questions to help you understand what is needed so you can be clear about how you can help and agree the purpose of the discussion
- Ask questions designed to help the other person think things through for themselves
- Listen for evidence of beliefs that could be challenged e.g. 'There's no point', 'He'll never agree', 'I can't do that'
- Gently seek evidence which supports or challenges the other person's beliefs
- Keep conscious focus on the purpose of the conversation
- Notice any thoughts/judgements/mind-wandering taking place within your own head and refocus on the other person, staying present in the moment
- Notice their body language, hear the words they are using and how they are speaking and reflect this back to them with curiosity.
- Help raise their self-awareness and help them identify what actions they could take to move things forward
- Check out with them if their proposed way forward is do-able and that they are committed to it
- End the conversation by noticing how you are feeling about the outcome. Check in with them how they feel too.

After the coaching conversation

Take some time to reflect on the conversation you've just had and ask yourself the following questions:

- How mindful did I remain throughout the conversation?
- What did I notice about my thoughts, my feelings, any physical sensations in my body?
- To what extent did I really listen to what the other person was saying?
- What judgements/distractions was I aware of in my own mind?

- To what extent did I get caught up in my own thoughts?
- How did I deal with these?
- How helpful was I in allowing the other person to think things through for themselves rather than offering suggestions/ideas/advice?

Summary

- **Start the coaching conversation by being fully present**
- **Engage fully in what the other person is saying through mindful listening**
- **Ask questions that enhance self-understanding**
- **Remain aware of your own thoughts, feelings and physical sensations**
- **Help move the other person towards their goals through questioning, not advising**

The Mindful Approach to

Influencing

Our ability to influence others in the workplace is one of the most important skills to develop in order to be effective at what we do. It affects our reputation and our career and yet most of the time it's not something we are consciously aware of. Being more mindful in how we influence is likely to have a positive impact on our work and the results we achieve. In order to understand what mindful influencing is, let's look at what mindful influencing isn't.

Lacking mindfulness when you are trying to influence someone may mean you:

- Fail to prepare properly
- Keep making your point in the same way or using variations on the same theme
- Don't really hear what the other person says because you are waiting for an opportunity to put your own point across
- Talk with passion but in an unfocused way
- Don't focus on what the other person's needs are
- Get into an argument
- Don't ask enough questions
- Avoid emotional connection
- Don't have clarity over what you are trying to achieve

Mindful influencing starts with being aware of yourself, of the other person, of how you are impacting the other person and the context in which the influencing is taking place.

Preparation

Sometimes people question whether planning, preparation, and thinking ahead are being mindful as these are future focused, not present focused activities. Planning and preparing mindfully means giving your full attention to future outcomes and noticing any reactions/thinking that arise when you do so.

You might be considering a future meeting with your line manager and wanting to influence her to allow you to be involved in a project. Preparing for this mindfully would mean observing the thoughts that arise during the planning process and remaining non-judgemental around the thoughts you have e.g. 'she might not think I'm experienced enough for this work'. Notice that you're thinking this; without mindfulness this thought could lead to a stream of consciousness of self-doubt or a defence of your abilities to yourself. With a more mindful approach, you can step back from the thought and reflect with consciousness and awareness the reality of your experience for this work.

Self awareness whilst influencing

To influence effectively, it's important to tune in to what's going on for you in the present moment; to be aware of what thoughts are going through your mind and the sensations you feel in your body.

Notice what's present for you, right here, right now. Settle yourself through focusing on the breath to fine tune your attention to the present. With a high level of presence, you are in an optimum position to be influential.

Mindful influencing also requires you to be aware of the messages you are projecting non-verbally to the other person. Emotions and thoughts such as disagreement, surprise, curiosity, boredom and interest can all be conveyed to the other person without you speaking a word. Being aware of what you are thinking and feeling in the moment allows you to express the messages you want them to see.

Awareness of the other person; listening and observing

Now turn your attention to the other person and be aware of them; what can you see? What can you hear? The key to being a successful influencer is your ability to genuinely listen to and observe the other person; their words, how they speak, their facial expressions and their body language. When you're truly listening to the other person, it's like there's a spotlight projected on them. If you get caught up in your own thinking, that spotlight shines on you instead. Keep the light on the person you're listening to and trust that in listening deeply you'll be able to respond appropriately and in a timely way.

Questioning

Some influencers don't ask enough questions of the other person and just 'tell' instead. This can provoke defensiveness in the other person and doesn't allow you to fully understand their perspective, thus limiting your ability to truly influence them. Mindful questioning follows the flow of the discussion and seeks to deepen the understanding of what's important to the person being influenced.

Language

Mindful influencers choose their words with care and consideration and are able to adapt their language to the style used by the other person. Flexibility is always important; to be able to draw on feelings, facts, statistics, examples, past experience or whatever is needed to effectively influence the other person.

Empathy

The practices of awareness, listening and questioning and using appropriate language will all help create empathy, which is the ability to understand and be sensitive towards the other person.

Managing your emotional response

Inevitably there will sometimes be conflict in influencing situations. Managing your emotions mindfully is important at this time (see The Mindful Approach to Regulating your emotions chapter Page 18) – as always it's about being observant, noticing what's going on internally and allowing the thinking/emotions without engagement.

Balancing 'push' and 'pull'

There are two main styles of influencing; the first is the 'push' approach which is focused on getting your objectives met by being strong, assertive and directive, essentially a 'tell' approach. This can be helpful when you're the expert and have clear and agreed logic on your side. It can also be experienced as being overly aggressive and uncollaborative.

The second style is the 'pull' approach which involves the other person more and increases the likelihood of joint agreement as it's based on listening and questioning to understand the other person's perspective and has an emphasis on finding common ground and creating a way forward together.

This can be helpful to build commitment and can often lead to a better solution; on the downside, it can be time-consuming and be experienced as lacking decisiveness.

The heart of mindful influencing

Adopting a mindful approach means weighing up which style is likely to work best for the situation you are facing and the people involved and be prepared to use each flexibly: It means speaking and listening with focused attention and noticing the impact you're having and adjusting your behaviour and style accordingly: It means not getting too hung up on who's right or judging the other person's perspective or behaviour and instead brings an approach of curiosity and present moment focus, combined with clarity about the end goal and openness to different ways of achieving it. At times there may need to be openness to changing the end goal too – being mindful throughout makes it more likely that you will see this as a possibility and an opportunity.

Influencing others more mindfully is always likely to be more successful than influencing someone using your 'autopilot - this is how I do it' way of operating. Like many workplace behaviours, influencing others can be enhanced dramatically by a more mindful approach.

Summary

- **Identify if you have any non-mindful influencing habits**
- **Think ahead to prepare how you intend to influence someone**
- **Notice what you're thinking and be aware of how you are coming across**
- **Bring full awareness to how you listen, what you say, how you say it**
- **Engage fully in what the other person says and how they say it**
- **Manage your feelings and how you respond in the moment**
- **Be flexible around adopting different 'push' and 'pull' styles of influencing**

The Mindful Approach to

Negotiations

Bringing a mindful approach to your negotiations can help you to notice new things that you were unaware of previously. It extends your awareness both of what's going on for you and the other party. Mindfulness practice is about being present, moment by moment. It is choosing to pay attention with an attitude of non-judgement and with a specific intention. Mindfulness can enable you to be more focused, less reactive, more open and able to build a better relationship, potentially leading to a better outcome overall to the negotiation.

Preparing to negotiate

Before you begin negotiating, take a moment to settle your mind. Find a quiet place to sit where you will not be disturbed. Notice what thoughts are present, what sensations are in your body, what emotions. How busy is your mind? Without judging what you are experiencing, gently turn your attention to your breath and follow the path of your breath as it enters into and exits your body. Simply following the breath, not controlling it. Notice what happens to the thoughts. Do they slow down? Become less? Flow in a pattern? Continue to follow the breath for a few more minutes. When you are ready to let go of following the breath, focus on an intention for the negotiation so that you can enter the meeting with a clear focus and feeling calm and in control.

It can be helpful to remember that the negotiation is not about you, it is about the situation, product, service. It's not about the other person either – it's about what you both want an outcome to be. Hold an image of yourself in your mind and silently say to yourself:

'May I feel safe, may I feel strong, may I feel calm, may I feel at ease'

Repeat these phrases a few times and notice what arises in your body and emotions. This is not about forcing yourself to be a certain way, it is an aspiration to be open to others.

Bring to mind an image of the people that you will be negotiating with and repeat the phrases silently:

'May you feel safe, may you feel strong; may you feel calm; may you feel at ease'

This practice helps to create a negotiating environment of mutual understanding where both parties seek to jointly problem solve, to build a relationship and to communicate with effectiveness.

Things to consider before the negotiation

It is good negotiations practice to consider:

What is your **ideal** outcome?

What is the **minimum** you are prepared to accept?

What do you **hope** to achieve?

What are you going to do if you fail to reach an agreement?

Mindful negotiation starts with being prepared, mentally and practically. The more prepared you are, the more likely you are to be able to respond calmly and rationally to what happens rather than an inappropriate ill-thought-through reaction.

During the negotiation

Give your full attention to the interaction and listen with awareness. See the chapter on The Mindful Approach to Conversations on Page 25 for more information.

Be open and curious throughout the meeting about whatever arises. Notice what sensations are in your body and your emotions. Let your body and emotions guide you in your responses. Just notice that you feel angry, frustrated, excited or optimistic. Do not try to analyse the emotion just make a mental note 'This is anger'. Take a mindful pause by placing your focus of attention on the sensations of your feet on the floor, your bottom on the chair. A few moments of practice in this way will give your mind and body a chance to reset so that you can see things more clearly and respond rather than react.

Learning conversations

Make the negotiation a learning conversation. Stay tuned into what the interests and concerns are for all present. As you hear comments and notice the response in your own body and feelings ask yourself, 'What needs to be addressed here?' Tune into your intuition and check what the concerns might be.

If you notice any tension in your body, again take a mindful pause and think about the fairness of the propositions being made. Is there anything that you need to address about the offer on the table?

Inner dialogues

At the height of negotiations when the stakes are high, there are often more voices in the room than there are people. During the conversation take regular moments to notice your own inner dialogue. We all have voices in our heads that are constantly telling us what we need to be doing or shouldn't be doing. Yours might sound like this:

'You're doing great. Nearly there. Well done!'

'That was a great comment.'

Or possibly, like this:

'What did you tell him that for?'

'That came out all wrong!'

'I'm looking nervous, don't show your feelings'

Notice your inner dialogue. Is it sabotaging your attempts to reach agreement? If you fail to be aware, what might you miss?

During the negotiation, consciously check in on your progress towards your ideal outcome/your hoped for solution/your minimum solution and whether it is time to agree a 'no deal' if the outcome you need can't be reached by both parties.

Ensure that there is clarity on the outcome; that there is a clear agreement in place. It can be tempting to rush the final stages as both parties are keen to agree a deal.

After the negotiation

Take a few moments to reflect. Check in with yourself how mindful you had been during the negotiation process. Allow feelings to surface and acknowledge them. Notice if there is anything that you can learn to help make the next negotiation more mindful and more effective.

Summary

- Take time to settle your mind before you negotiate
- Be clear on the outcome that you are looking for
- Seek to build a relationship, be compassionate and look for mutual understanding
- Give your full attention and listen with awareness
- Take mindful pauses when you notice any tension in your mind, body, emotions
- Ensure there is clarity on the outcomes agreed

The Mindful Approach to

Feedback

Arguably, feedback is one of the most effective ways of helping someone learn, develop and grow. It can also be uncomfortable to give and awkward to receive. This can mean that feedback is often avoided or handled badly and, if offered, can be received with defensiveness or denial. It's a potential minefield for both parties, so this chapter addresses how to give and receive feedback in a mindful way, enabling the giver and the receiver to benefit from the interaction.

Before you offer feedback

Whether it's 'in the moment' or planned feedback, for instance as part of a performance review, take a moment to reflect on your intention behind offering the feedback. Take three conscious breaths to focus your attention. What are you trying to achieve? To improve someone's performance? If so why? Beware of offering someone feedback because they don't do things like you do! Is it to help raise their self-awareness and, if so, in order to do what? Check your motives aren't selfish; to get something off your chest; to make you feel better. Notice any thoughts, feelings or physical sensations and any desire to wound or hurt the other person because you believe at some level they deserve to be punished for something they have done or failed to do. Be fully aware of the purpose of your feedback and what you want the outcome to be.

Choose your moment

As part of your self-reflection, if you uncover motivations that undermine what you are objectively trying to achieve, then gently challenge the need to give feedback at this time. Instead, choose a time when your self-reflection reveals a desire to help the other person learn, develop or grow. The more aware you are of your own intentions and the more you ensure those intentions are about helping the other person to behave or perform better, the more mindful you are in engaging in the feedback.

Assuming your intentions are positive and are to help the development of the other person, find a time and location that are suitable for someone to hear your perspective on their performance. Ideally it's best to deliver feedback, whether it's positive or negative, as soon as possible after the event you have observed as long as you are able to give the feedback in an emotionally neutral way. Before you do give feedback, check that you feel calm, that you have the facts and that you are able to articulate your perspective with respect for the other person.

Giving feedback

- Describe the **Situation** you have observed with as much detail as possible
- Describe the **Behaviour** you have observed, without evaluation or judgement
- Describe the **Impact** it had on you/perceived impact on others

Agree what needs to change (if anything); this can be through questioning the individual or suggesting an alternative response.

For example, 'In today's meeting I noticed you checking your phone on multiple occasions, and texting on a couple of occasions. You're normally a good contributor to these meetings but on this occasion, you made no comments. I'm concerned that you weren't fully engaged in the meeting; you seemed distracted by your phone. What was going on? What needs to happen for you to be fully engaged and contributing well at the next meeting?'

'In today's meeting, I noticed that you made your point really articulately and passionately about the forthcoming changes; everyone around the table was engaged in what you were saying and it provoked a healthy debate where you remained calm and yet still passionate. I really admire your passion and your ability to project this with confidence – well done!'

Keep emotional control

As you share your observations, it's important to retain emotional control even when you are expressing strong feelings. It's perfectly OK to express frustration, anger, pride or delight for example, and do so from a mindful perspective, being aware of how you are coming across to the other person and also aware of how they are receiving your message.

Retaining emotional control is also important as they respond, especially if the message has been a difficult one for them to hear. Notice any response in yourself as you listen to them and observe them; notice how your body reacts and the thoughts that spring into your mind. Allow the thoughts and sensations to pass through without engaging with them.

Receiving feedback

Being on the receiving end of feedback tends to promote an emotional response which may be any of a range of emotions and sometimes conflicting emotions (e.g. delight/embarrassed). Feedback may not be an accurate reflection of how you see yourself; it is however an accurate reflection of how you're perceived.

Listen non-defensively

When you find yourself on the receiving end of feedback, listen carefully to what's being said and be open to the other person's perspective without dismissing it or getting defensive about it. Even positive feedback can be dismissed sometimes out of disbelief or embarrassment. If you find yourself feeling dismissive or defensive, acknowledge those feelings in yourself and allow yourself to be curious instead, probing more deeply if something seems unclear or unfair.

Thank the individual who has shared the feedback with you and let them know how you intend to use the information (if this is appropriate) and you may wish to seek out alternative perspectives to better understand if the highlighted issue impacts others as well.

The importance of balance in feedback

Research by Losada indicated that in high performing teams there were almost six times as many positive comments as negative ones. Gottmann discovered that in happy couples, there are five times as many positive comments as negative ones. This research would indicate that colleagues who receive more positive feedback than negative are more likely to thrive than the reverse. A culture of feedback-giving in a mindful and respectful way, where feedback is received similarly, is the recipe for growth and development. Add to this, colleagues who sincerely notice and comment on one another's positive behaviours at a ratio of at least 3:1 (research by Barbara Fredrickson) then the culture is highly likely to encourage high performance and flourishing team members.

Feedback is an essential tool that can support development, bring about changes and even enhance motivation if delivered and received in a mindful way. Most people say they don't get enough feedback and would welcome more so they are clear how they are perceived by others and how well they are doing. Take a deep breath, focus your attention and intention, offer your observations, and invite a response.

Summary

- **Notice the intention behind your feedback**
- **Carefully choose the time and place**
- **Describe the behaviour objectively and its impact**
- **Keep control of your emotions**
- **Be non-defensive when hearing feedback**
- **Seek out and offer positive feedback more consistently than negative**

The Mindful Approach to

Performance management

The formal performance management process is often viewed by both managers and their direct reports as a time wasting activity that no one sets any real importance by. Comments such as these are typical:

'My manager never listens anyway'

'Its aim is to fit the bell curve so why try?'

'This is just a tick box exercise'

'My manager doesn't know what I do. My day is spent doing work in another department!'

Even as a manager, responsible for the process, you may be wishing you could spend your time doing 'real work' or something more useful.

Whilst these views are understandable, given the negative experience many of us have with the assessment and development process, this kind of thinking and the mind set it creates sets the performance management process up to fail before it's begun.

What is mindful performance management?

Mindful performance management allows all parties to see the process in a different way; as a more meaningful process to give direction and focus; as an opportunity to have an honest and helpful discussion about past and desired future performance that is motivational to both manager and individual.

So how do you approach performance management in a mindful way?

Before the review

Whether you are the manager or the individual, take time to notice how you are feeling about the performance management process, mentally and physically. Take a minute to be aware, not altering your experience just accepting it for now.

Move your attention to your breathing and take ten breaths; as thoughts arise just notice the thoughts and gently bring your focus and attention back to the breath.

Now bring all of your attention and focus to the question: 'What is the purpose of performance management, for the manager, for the individual, for the organisation?'

Notice how your answers make you feel. What can you do differently to make the experience an effective and beneficial one? Maybe thinking about how the process can allow you to recognise your or your direct report's achievements and have the opportunity to celebrate these. Maybe thinking about how honest feedback can boost confidence and highlight future areas for development or growth. How might you approach the mid-year review or end of year review differently with this aim in mind?

As well as preparing yourself to approach this session with positive intent, it's essential to take time to review your achievements throughout the year (or if you are the manager, the achievements of your direct report). Gather evidence of effort, results, feedback; anything that allows for a complete review of how things have gone. Most people (managers and those being appraised alike) do not spend sufficient time preparing for performance management discussions. The more prepared both parties are, the higher the potential for quality discussion.

Just prior to the session take a few minutes to pay attention to how you are feeling, what is here right now for you? Do not judge your feelings at this time, simply acknowledge them. This 'checking in' allows you to be fully present with your attention in the moment and more able to engage fully in the process.

During the review

The performance management review session is an opportunity to reflect on the past and learn from it; this means celebrating the successes and tackling poor performance with honesty and sensitivity.

Key skills are listening, questioning, challenging and supporting, all of which can be done mindfully.

Heightened observational skills are also needed for a mindful performance review, note what's going on inside you, watch the body language and listen to clues offered by how the other person is speaking.

It can be hard to stay in the moment in these kind of discussions. Be aware of when your mind wanders. What thoughts are present? Are they based on past events and beliefs? Is your mind leaping forward in time and creating false pictures about reality? Stay in the moment, notice how you are feeling. Listen to what is being said and how it is being communicated. Listen to how you are responding. Stay present.

If the session sparks emotions in you, notice the feeling. Label the feeling inwardly. Use the feeling to guide you in whether to simply sit with it or mention it so that you're able to continue to focus on the conversation.

If the conversation feels difficult, focus your attention on your breath. Using the in breath and the out breath as an anchor to keep you present.

At the end of the review

As the review draws to a close, it's important that both parties feel listened to and understood and the person being appraised has a clear understanding of his/her performance and what may need to be developed for the future. A mindful performance review presents the opportunity for enhanced mutual understanding and a closer working relationship; also important is clarity of understanding what's happened and what needs to happen and commitment to what's been discussed. Take the opportunity to check in at the end that this has been achieved.

What if you approach the performance management process mindfully but your manager or direct report does not?

In an ideal world, both manager and the person being reviewed would approach the discussion from a mindful perspective, but this may not be the reality in your organisation. Core to mindfulness is acceptance and non-judgement of others and this is what's needed in this situation. If you do your best to stay present, notice what's going on for you and the other person and focus on the quality of the attention you bring to the discussion, then this will lead to a better experience for both people. Chances are, your mindful state will have a beneficial impact on your manager/direct report too.

Summary

- **Prepare by using the breath to be present**
- **Ensure you have all of your evidence of effort and results ready**
- **During the review, notice how you are feeling, thinking, acting and take mindful pauses to bring your awareness into the moment**
- **Use the breath as an anchor to enable you to respond appropriately and effectively**
- **Check what has been understood and achieved at the end of the review**
- **Be compassionate**

The Mindful Approach to

Motivating yourself and others

Sometimes it's a general lack of motivation that affects us; feeling like everything takes effort. Sometimes it's motivation to achieve a particular goal; make a big change; deliver a project or tackle an issue that we've been putting off. Sometimes it's about identifying how to motivate someone else whose lack of motivation is having a negative impact on us: whatever your reason, a mindful approach to motivation will optimise your chances of a successful outcome.

Set aside some time to consider the issue. In a quiet environment, take a three step breathing space (See Appendix Page 118) to bring yourself fully to the present moment. Notice if your mind is already thinking ahead to the issues you want to explore and potential solutions. If it does, gently refocus on the breath and your current experience in the here and now.

Motivating yourself

What excuses are you making?

Motivation starts with you taking responsibility for the decisions you make and the actions you take. Tune into your current thinking and identify what excuses you are giving yourself. Are the excuses about

- Your circumstances?
- Other people?
- How you feel?
- The demands made on your time?

Capture your list of excuses and simply accept that this is how you are currently experiencing your life. This is how it is right now. Be compassionate with yourself; no judgement.

What needs to be done?

Identify what needs doing; the big things, the little things and look at the level of effort to achieve them and the level of reward once achieved. Think of the benefits of doing these things and of the implications if you don't do them Some people are more motivated by thinking of the benefits of achieving goals; others are more motivated by thinking about the negative consequences if the goals aren't met: both are legitimate motivation strategies.

What's really important to you?

Now it's time to connect with what's really important to you; your values, and how you'll feel once the tasks are completed. How does achieving your goals connect to what you value most deeply? Sometimes a lack of motivation comes from a disconnection between what we need to do and how it connects to what is important to us in life.

What is it that really matters to you at work? Is it making a difference/achieving/results/business/success/developing people/adding to the bottom line/accomplishing goals etc? Think in a conscious and considered way about the connections between what you need to do and what is fundamentally important to you.

If you are more motivated by the negative consequences if things don't get done, then consider how you may fail to make a difference/not get the results you want/business failure/failing to help people develop/not adding value to the bottom line/failing to achieve goals etc.

As you consider the above, do so mindfully by paying attention to the thoughts that come into your mind and observing them without judgement. Do not get caught up in the trail of thoughts, simply notice each thought, note it and let it go. Stay focused on your intention of uncovering what needs doing, how you will feel once the task is completed and the impact that the outcomes have on what's important to you, whether positive or negative.

Taking action in the moment of choice

Having spent time thinking through your intentions, now it is time to consider what you do in the moment of choice, that moment when you have the opportunity to choose whether you work towards your goals or not. Again, being mindful can really help here. Be conscious of the choice you make when you have a decision point about what to focus on. Make a considered decision in the light of your thinking above – be mindful rather than working on auto-pilot.

Making a start

Sometimes making a start is the hardest part because we build something up in our minds to be enormous when in reality every task can be broken down into small steps. What's the smallest first step you could take? Could you commit to fifteen minutes on something? Just making a start can motivate us to continue. Sometimes we put off starting something because we kid ourselves we will feel more like doing it at some point in the future. Sometimes, we can't feel motivated at first, we just have to get on and do it.

Motivating yourself to achieve a challenging, specific goal

Preparing for success

As you answer the questions below, do so with awareness and focus, noticing any tendencies for your thoughts to wander off course. Once you become aware of your thinking wandering off, take a breath and re-focus.

- Write down your goal, expressed in positive terms and the reasons why you want to achieve it
- Are there any downsides to you achieving this goal? What can you do about these?
- Ask yourself if you really believe you can do it: How confident are you of success?
- If you have any doubts, write down what they are and how you will tackle them
- Project yourself into the future and write down all the reasons why you've been successful
- Project yourself into the future and write down all the reasons why you've failed
- What can you do to optimise your chances of success and reduce your chances of failure?
- Ask yourself, if you've been unsuccessful in the past, what's going to be different this time?
- Ask yourself, what are the consequences of you not achieving this goal?
- Plan your deadline for achieving your goal, sub goals and what actions you are going to take and when

Going through the above thinking and planning process will encourage you to be more mindful of what you are aiming to do and the challenges you're facing. It enables you to consider all aspects of the goal and how you set about achieving it. It enables you to be prepared for difficulties you may encounter and to optimise your chances of success.

Take action

- Monitor your progress on an ongoing basis, learning from things that have gone well and things that haven't
- Get support from other people
- Learn from others who have achieved similar goals
- Be conscious of how your present actions affect your future goals
- Treat any setbacks as part of the process; press pause, review and move on
- Be really clear what you can control and what you can't; make considered decisions and take personal responsibility for those decisions
- Take time to notice how you are moving forward towards your goal.
- Celebrate your progress!

Motivating others

Many people think that money is the prime motivating factor for someone at work. Research has shown it is more complex than this and reward ceases to be a motivating factor when we are paid our market worth and are satisfied in our roles. Human motivation is also likely to include some aspects of the following:

Key motivators

- A sense of achievement
- Challenge
- Recognition
- Autonomy/control
- A sense of personal growth
- Meaning/purpose
- Inspiration
- Belonging

- Attention
- Reward

Taking time to learn about what truly motivates someone

Taking a more mindful approach encourages us to challenge any assumptions we are making about what motivates other people.

Take time to find out what is important to the individuals you want to motivate. Engage in a mindful conversation with them: Talk to them, think about their behaviour. Ask them to talk about occasions when they have done their best work. What drives them? What enables them to perform at their best? They may be aware of what's important to them, they may not. Help them uncover their own motivations.

Creating the conditions for the success of others

Help them to get what they need as individuals; be observant of what works for them. Help them to see the vision of what's possible or the downside of failure.

Offer the right balance of support and challenge and always offer feedback on a regular and timely basis ensuring you highlight the positives of their effort and achievement as well as any aspects that still need improvement.

Mindful motivation of others encourages you to question your own assumptions about what motivates someone and asks you instead to be observant, sensitive and respectful of what's important to them, giving them scope to experience what allows them to perform at their best.

Summary
- **Notice your excuses**
- **Consciously decide what's most important**
- **Be aware of your choice in the moment**
- **Make a start**
- **Consider all the factors that motivate someone**
- **Deepen your understanding of the individual**
- **Create the conditions for the success of others**

The Mindful Approach to

Change

One of the best truisms is that change is a constant. Change is a natural part of life and inevitable. So how do you feel about the changes that take place in your life? Do you embrace change or do you find it difficult to accept change? In this chapter we share some strategies that will help you to manage change more effectively whether it's the changes that you are facing or taking your team or organisation through a change initiative.

Change is exponential

We live in an age of exponential change - never before have we experienced changes in our lives at so many levels and at such a pace. In your market sector, organisation, teams, people will have work and life circumstances that require adjusting to in knowledge, skills, behaviours and emotions. Take a moment to reflect on the changes that you have experienced over the past year. These may include changes at work in initiatives, products, process, management, leadership, colleagues. Include changes at home such as children growing up, births, deaths, illness, changes in wealth, friendships, moving house, decorating. Change is a fact of life and the way that you view change can have a significant impact on your health and wellbeing.

Accept impermanence

Name one thing in life that is static, non-changing, in any shape or form. Look at nature: mountains erode, landscapes evolve, all living forms change at a cellular level. We cannot stop change happening and so it is important that we learn how to embrace and manage those changes that take place in our life and work.

Maybe you love change and see it as opportunity. On the other hand, perhaps enjoyment of security and certainty means that for you change is a stressor. Quite often it is the changes that are imposed on us, the ones that we don't choose, that are the ones that we struggle with the most, for example redundancy, poor health, new bosses.

'Fear, uncertainty and discomfort are your compasses toward growth.'
Unknown author

Thoughts shape emotions

How you think about the changes that happen at work has a direct impact on how you feel. If you think that the changes are good and necessary, will save jobs, grow the business, provide financial security, then you may be more likely to embrace the changes. On the other hand if you see them as threatening, increasing your work load, decreasing your resources or increasing risk of losing your job, then you may start to experience a whole range of emotions from anger to sadness. There is a direct link between how we think, what we feel and our actions and behaviours. If we are able to learn to think differently about the changes we are experiencing then we can take different actions.

The 'what if game...'

Let's look at a couple of scenarios about thinking patterns. Your manager announces that over the next quarter there will be some restructuring required and further information will be communicated shortly. Do you start to play the 'What if...' game?

'What if I lose my job?'

'What if my team is decimated?'

'What if my work load increases and I lose my work/life balance?'

'What if my friends and colleagues are made redundant?'

It's easy to get caught up in this internal dialogue of playing the 'What if...' game, and at this point the change has yet to happen. A lot of stress can be created through this way of thinking when perhaps there doesn't need to be. When we feel stressed it's hard to think clearly, it's hard to be positive and the chemicals secreted by our brains actually slow down the ability to react rationally.

Change: An emotional roller coaster

Studies have shown that with any change we experience a range of emotions that can be grouped into four stages. For change to be successful we need to move through each of the four stages. Some people move through very quickly and others get stuck at points. It's useful to have an appreciation of which stage you or your team is in and how to move through these stages from the ending of something that you have, to a new beginning, a new situation. The four stages of the change are:

- **Stage 1: Shock, denial** – not feeling ready to make the change, worrying about the personal impact. If you are at this stage you will need support from colleagues, managers, friends as you seek to understand where your skills and knowledge fit in the change and what you need to do. Notice your feelings and accept these, even though they may feel uncomfortable.

- **Stage 2: Blame, anger**- once the shock has worn off you may feel the need to express your feelings. It is useful to remember at this stage that the change is not aimed at you personally. Mindfulness will help you to notice your feelings and your thoughts and not get caught up in negative thinking. If you are at this stage, take time to focus on your breathing or do a body scan (See Appendix Page 119) to help gain clarity and improve your decision making. If you are managing teams through the change then bringing mindfulness into the process will enable you to react with compassion and empathy, to ensure that people have the information that they need and that, importantly, they feel heard.

- **Stage 3: Uncertainty** – at this stage you may have questions and be trying to make sense of how things work. This can be a danger zone if not handled correctly with people moving back to stage 2 instead of onwards to stage 4. If you are here then take the time to notice what those thoughts are that you are having. Put your questions and concerns in writing to get a more objective view. Maybe take ten breaths to help you gain clarity and put you in control of the choices that you might make. Ask for more information and detail on the changes, the benefits and the future plans.

- **Stage 4: Acceptance and commitment** – by this stage, you have come to terms with the changes and will have started to adapt and adjust. Be observant of your thoughts and feelings and compassionate to self and others as the changed situation becomes more familiar.

Change the thoughts

Throughout the change process, being aware of your inner dialogue - the thoughts that you are having - can help you to take control of your thoughts and change feelings of being concerned, worried, or powerless to feeling empowered, energised and more confident. For example:

- 'What if I lose my job?' Changes to 'What do I need to do to be ready for that possibility?'
- 'What if my team are decimated?' Changes to 'Realistically what resource capacity will I need to manage the current levels of demands?'
- 'What if my work load increases and I lose my work/life balance?' Changes to 'What do I need to discuss with my manager to ensure that the work load is manageable and that I have the right skills for the role?'
- 'What if my friends and colleagues are made redundant?' Changes to 'How can I support my friends through transition and what do I need to do to maintain my engagement and motivation?'

Creating scenarios in your head that have not happened yet and possibly never will is not going to be helpful. The first step is to notice those thoughts. Mindfulness helps you to pay attention to your thoughts without getting caught up in them.

Practicing mindfulness daily through the change process will help you to be aware of how you think and how often you are lost in the narrative of negative thoughts. This awareness will help you to take control, to make choices, ask questions and start to move forward on the change curve to commitments that you need and want to make.

Mindfulness can help with the awareness of thoughts and feelings and with this awareness it is easier to be able to make more effective decisions.

Strategies for change

Here are a few strategies for using in those moments that range from a career-changing announcement being made to being caught in a stream of worry about possible consequences:

- **Focus your attention on your body**. Do a body scan. Take your attention, as if it was a spotlight, and bring it down your body into your legs, into both feet and all the way out to your toes and notice what you are feeling; any tensions or tightness. Just notice the effect that the situation is having on you physically. Turn your attention to your breathing. Follow the path of the in-breath into your abdomen, feeling your abdomen inflate and deflate on the out-breath. After a minute bring your awareness to the whole of your body - as if the whole of your body was breathing and notice any sensations that are here now. Be ready to take action and deal with the situation.
- **Take a walk and focus on your walking** by bringing your attention to the motion of walking, the sensation of your feet connecting with the ground and leaving the ground to take another step. Notice where your breathing is, in the abdomen, the chest, fast or slow. Just notice. After a few minutes of walking, stop and be aware of the sensations in your body. Repeat until your mind is clearer, you are more fully present and able to manage the situation.
- **It can be helpful to sit and be mindful for ten minutes**, just breathing (See Appendix Page 117). The second step, when the ten minutes are finished, write down the thoughts that you noticed on a piece of paper with two columns; one column labelled Positive Thoughts and the other labelled Negative Thoughts. What do you notice about the balance of positive thoughts to negative thoughts? The third step is to change any negative thoughts into positive ones as described in 'Change the thoughts' above. The fourth step may be to prepare a list of questions that you have about the change. What do you need to know that can help you to think about your situation differently?

Summary
- **Change is inevitable; find a way to accept the changes**
- **Choose thoughts that empower you**
- **Focus on the present moment by using your breath as an anchor**
- **Ask yourself 'What do I need to do?' and 'What do I need to know?'**

The Mindful Approach to

Networking

Whilst a great deal of networking can be done on line, there is a real benefit to networking in person, whether it's inside or outside of your organisation. Internally or externally, networking enables you to make connections, build relationships, get questions answered, help someone else, garner support for your ideas, get updates or position yourself for future opportunities. Mindful networking is about being purposeful, paying attention to your needs and the needs of the other person and bringing your full awareness to the interaction.

It's easy to treat networking as something you 'should' be doing. Or it's something you'll get round to in the future when things quieten down. Or you have a burst of networking because you fear for your job but once the danger has passed, you no longer consider networking a priority.

Keeping and nurturing networks is better seen as a conscious and ongoing process, simply part of the way you work. In reality, networking is an important part of a working career. Networking creates opportunity at many levels. The opportunity to meet new people; to learn from others; to grow your personal brand, reputation and credibility; to connect with other people; to help others too. Mindful networking starts with the intention to network.

Your networking approach

Consider your current network - who you know in positions of influence or who have information or expertise in your area? Think about these people and the strength of your relationship with them. Notice how you feel about them as you bring them to mind. Which relationships need your attention at the moment and what might be your intention in nurturing these relationships? Networking should always be about mutual benefit; sharing of ideas and information that is helpful to both parties. Think broadly about how developing your network can benefit you; getting you access to information, expertise, advice, influence. Bring to mind an intention for networking that focuses on cooperation, collaboration and mutually beneficial outcomes. Recognise how important it is for you in your career at this time.

Mindful networking tips

- Make a conscious effort to stay in touch with people you have worked with in the past. Who might it be worthwhile re-connecting with?
- As you meet people during your day to day working life, engage fully in these contacts and actively identify people who could help you or people who you could help
- Identify gaps in your network and seek out opportunities to plug these gaps through attending meetings or events which key people may attend
- It's OK to ask for help or to ask to be introduced to someone. Express gratitude for any help offered
- Be proactive about helping people out - it's easier to build a network through giving rather than taking
- Be selective about who you choose to network with - whilst a broad network can be desirable, a focused network that is well nurtured is best
- When you engage with a networking contact, give them your full attention. Pay attention to them, be curious about them, listen wholeheartedly and deeply. See the chapter on Mindful Conversations (Page 25) for more information.

Formal networking events

Attending networking events can feel like a daunting prospect with the thought that you may have to spend a few hours in mindless small talk, talking to complete strangers and handing out and collecting business cards from people who you probably will not see again!

Perhaps if we took away the 'working' part of the activity we might approach these events as enjoyable, socialising events.

Whether your networking event is the company sales conference; a large event organized by a professional body or a client, your attitude will determine how successful it is for you. If you attend with an attitude of ambivalence; annoyance; fear; shyness; arrogance, impatience and the chances are you will get the results that perpetuate your beliefs about networking being a waste of time.

What are your experiences of networking?

- I have nothing to say to people
- Everyone is busy selling themselves
- It's artificial and I have to 'perform'

Notice your thoughts about networking. Realise that these are just thoughts, not your reality. Just because you think it doesn't mean it's true. Let the thoughts pass without judgement and focus on your intention.

Eight steps to mindful networking at a formal event:

Step 1: Set a goal

What is your intention for attending the networking event? Are there particular people that you want to meet? Why do you want to meet them? What do you want them to know about you or what do you want to know about them? What is the impression that you wish to create? How are you going to be; talkative; knowledgeable; intense; relaxed; sociable? How many people do you want to introduce yourself to?

Having a goal will give you a focus for the event and if networking is something that you find hard to do then being focused on what you want to achieve will help. As you decide what's important for you to achieve at the event, breathe deeply as you connect to your purpose.

Step 2: Prepare some questions

Successful networkers advocate having a bank of questions that you can use to open up the conversation. Some examples are:

'What is on your reading list at the moment?'

'What made you decide to come to this event?'

'Tell me about what you do'

'What do you think about the event?'

Consider what questions you would genuinely like to hear the answer to.

Step 3: Mentally rehearse

It helps to think of networking as a means of connecting with other people. How do we successfully connect with other people? We show genuine interest, compassion, respect for them and we listen to what they have to say. Take a few moments before leaving for the event, or in your car, to picture yourself meeting and talking to people at the event. Notice how you feel in your body and emotions as you play that video in your mind. How is your body language and tone of voice? Imagine you saying one of your opening questions and being genuinely interested in the response you receive back.

Step 4: Set the intention to be attentive

As you enter the room move up the gears in your mindfulness practice. Be present, notice what is happening around you. Who is in the room? What does the atmosphere feel like? Use your social awareness skills to full effect. Putting your attention on what is present will distract your mind from your own thoughts and feelings enough for you to notice what people are saying and doing. You will be surprised by what you notice about other people when your thoughts are more on them than on yourself.

Step 5: Making connections

Our emotions play a big part in our interactions with others. Take a few breaths and notice whether your mood is good, bad, light, nervous, bored, excited. As you pay attention to your mood, simply accept however you are feeling. Manage any negative inner chatter about what people may be thinking about you. Be aware of your thoughts and your feelings, just noticing them and not getting caught up in them. Focus on following the path of your breath for a few breaths whilst your emotions settle and allow you to be fully present in the room. Recall your image of enjoying conversations with people socially.

Step 6: Introduce yourself

A good technique for making connections with others is to genuinely focus on the other person. Be fully present as you shake their hand, look them in the eyes and say your first and last name. Be attentive, tune into noticing all you can about them, with a positive intention. Notice how they look; their body language; the tone of their voice; the words they choose. When you ask a question, fully engage with the individual, give them your complete attention at a level well beyond how you might typically engage when in a 'small talk' type conversation. Aim to connect with them deeply and fully even if only for a few minutes.

What might they be feeling as they talk? What is their intention behind the words you are hearing? What can you learn about this person? Make them feel listened to. When we talk to someone in this way they feel respected and valued as a person. Giving someone our time, energy and attention makes them feel good and they are more likely to remember you.

Step 7: Think about giving

Instead of thinking about what you can personally gain from networking, think about networking as an opportunity to give to others. Think about how you can meet other people's needs. Perhaps you have connections that they would benefit from. Offer to introduce them to people who you know. Listen to learn about them and to understand what their needs are.

Step 8: Follow up

Back at the office, drop an email to the people that you met with whom you would like to stay in touch Share a piece of information; invite them to connect with you on social media such as Twitter, Facebook or LinkedIn. These methods of communication will help you to continue to stay connected and to share information with each other.

Summary

- **Create a mind-set around networking that is positive and worthwhile**
- **Choose to network with an approach that seeks mutual benefit**
- **Give people your full attention**
- **Think how you can genuinely be helpful to others**

The Mindful Approach to

Politics

As coaches working with professionals and executives, the word 'politics' often comes up in our discussions and is often accompanied by a grimace on the part of our clients! You may be aware of a political climate at work and think all politics are best avoided or be unsure how to engage in a way that is helpful to you and the organisation where you work. The reality is though, politics is widespread in organisations and it can be hard to do your job successfully without an understanding of how to manage and make the most of the political climate.

When we talk about mindful politics in this chapter, we are certainly not advocating mindful backstabbing, mindful manipulation, or promoting yourself excessively in a mindful way!

Negative vs positive politics

Mark Holden, in his book, *The use and abuse of office politics* talks about negative politics, namely, 'the manipulation of the behaviour of others with the sole purpose of achieving personal gain at the expense of individual or organisational goals' and positive politics, 'the ability to influence the behaviour of others with the purpose of achieving the shared goals of the individuals involved as well as those of the organisation'.

Our focus here is on helping you to become more mindful in positive politics and build on The Mindful Approach to Influencing chapter (Page 75). It's helpful to elevate politics to a more conscious act, rather than something engaged in (or indeed not engaged in) without due thought or awareness as this is where it's more likely to be misconstrued as being negative.

Why engage in positive political behaviour? It:

- Gives you the opportunity to promote your work and your team's work to key stakeholders, raising your visibility
- Can help you access useful information about what's going on in the organisation
- Can give insight into opportunities available
- Can help you get your work done more efficiently and effectively

Competence, confidence and self-promotion

Mindful politics starts with you doing a good job, being credible at what you do and being able to talk positively about your ability to other people. It requires you to believe in yourself and be comfortable standing up for yourself and your abilities. Being mindfully political also invites you to assess your weaker aspects and work on these, without drawing too much attention to them, allowing your real strengths to shine through. Engaging mindfully in this allows you to get the balance right between being overly modest and overly arrogant. You must be willing to talk about your successes, as appropriate, to the people who need to hear about your successes and you need to be able to identify who these people are. This is about identifying key individuals and ensuring that you manage your reputation with these stakeholders.

You're aiming for positive self-promotion based on a realistic assessment of your contribution plus an open acceptance of where you still need to develop. What we're looking for here is, 'I'm delighted that my presentation to the board was so well received and I know there's still the HR Director that I need to work on' rather than, 'that was awful – the HR Director made mincemeat of me!'

Trust

If you are to be able to navigate politics successfully within an organisation, you need to be both trusted and able to trust others. A mindful approach will facilitate the development of trust. Trust is gained or lost according to how people perceive your intentions and your actions. You can build trust by:

Delivering on your commitments

If you consider things from a mindful perspective, you are more likely to consider the implications of taking on work before you commit and therefore more likely to make a realistic assessment of your ability to deliver.

Being open

Being open with people is a proven way to build positive relationships as long as that openness is appropriate. The best way to consider the appropriateness of sharing information is to pause and reflect on how the information may be received before proceeding (or not).

Being fair

Fairness is not an absolute and therefore once again the need to pause, check, reflect before making a statement or making a decision will improve your ability to get it right more often.

Reputation and relationships

You have a reputation at work, whether or not you have consciously cultivated it. Take a moment to reflect on how you would be described by your team, peers, those senior to you in the organisation, customers, suppliers. What about the receptionist? Every interaction you have with someone at work is an opportunity to build (or otherwise!) your reputation. Bring mindfulness to your interactions and your relationships with stakeholders and you bring your full attention, your ability to notice how you are impacting on them and your ability to adjust your style accordingly. Being positively political is ultimately all about building relationships with integrity, mutual trust and mutual respect; being friendly across all levels of the organisation. Mindfulness brings awareness and presence and with it the ability to invest in the relationships that matter.

Attitude and behaviour

A mindful approach enables you to observe what's going on in the organisation, picking up the undercurrents, noticing who has influence and respect and the relationship dynamics at play. In mindfulness, you learn to pay attention and to take a non-judgemental approach. In the workplace, this translates as being observant, acting with integrity with regard to self and the organisation, being non-judgemental of others, rising above the office gossip and taking the organisational perspective when it comes to conflict, rather than putting your own needs first.

Dealing with other people's negative politics

If being mindful means being in the present moment, with awareness and without judgement, then there is a wonderful opportunity to be mindful when you become aware of the shady dealings of others. When negative thoughts about self or others come into your awareness, you have a choice; to engage with the thinking or to allow the thoughts to pass. Mindfulness is not about ignoring negative thoughts, it's about noticing them and making a decision from a clearer perspective how to handle the thoughts. So notice your thinking which has been prompted by your interpretation of something that's happened; be a witness to your thinking.

Compassion for self and others is closely aligned to mindfulness. As you notice your thinking and the tendency to judge the other person's actions or intentions, take a moment to breathe to get a moment of clarity. Now is the time to act with conscious awareness, to consider how you yourself feel and to decide if now is the best time to respond or if it's best to let things settle. It's important that if you choose to let things settle, you do not replay what's upset you over and over in your mind, trying to make sense of it.

Be polite to people engaged in negative politics and be careful of what you disclose to them. Try to understand what motivates their behaviour rather than judge them for using it. Your understanding will enhance your ability to manage their behaviour and mitigate its impact on you and your team.

Take a moment to reflect on this chapter mindfully by finding a quiet place to practice the three step breathing space, described in the Appendix (Page 118). Allow your mind to reflect for a few minutes on your mindful approach to politics. What can you change? What one thing can you do today to enhance your impact?

Summary

- **Be prepared to approach politics from a mindful perspective**
- **Consider what's best for you, your team and organisation**
- **Endeavour to build trust with others through being open, fair and getting the job done**
- **Manage your reputation through cultivating positive interactions with others**
- **Notice what's going on in the organisation and be aware of how you engage in conversations about this**
- **Manage judgement of others, cultivate compassion and disclose your thoughts and ideas with care**

The Mindful Approach to

Balancing your life

An ongoing challenge of the technologically driven times we live in is to get the right balance for us between the hours we work and the hours we dedicate to non-work activities. No longer is there a simple dividing line between work and home, the boundaries are more blurred for many professionals. It can end up as a constant battle of work vs non work activities, each competing for the limited time available. This can often lead to a sense of dissatisfaction with both or unwelcome compromises being made, which ultimately breed a sense of guilt and under-accomplishment in one or both areas of life.

How a more mindful focus can lead to better choices

There are issues around the choices we make during the day about where to focus time and energy and then there's the issue with how we feel about these choices. Getting the right balance means looking at the choices we make on a day by day basis and examining how we think and feel about those choices. A mindful approach can help with the moment by moment choices and the thinking/feeling about the choices made.

Creating a vision for balance

The starting point is to look at what would getting the right balance for you mean in practical terms at work and home. Take some time to reflect on this. Treat this reflection time as a mindful exercise in itself. Start by focusing your attention on your breath for a few moments and settle into yourself by noticing how your body connects to where you are sitting. Be purposeful in your reflection as you consider:

- What would I be doing if my life was balanced to meet my work and non-work needs?
- What wouldn't I be doing?
- What would I be thinking?
- What would I be feeling?

Now ask yourself if your vision is achievable given your current circumstances.

Whether the answer is yes or no, what steps could you take to move yourself closer to your goal?

Some examples of practical steps to take:

- Take a short break every 90 minutes
- Plan your priorities at the beginning of each day
- Leave an hour a day unscheduled to allow for non-planned-for work
- Allow yourself the last 15 minutes of each day and take time to reflect on the day and plan for the next
- Only attend meetings that are essential for you to attend.
- Notice any feelings of guilt, label them, 'here's guilt' and let them pass you by
- Do not look at work emails once you have left the office or after 7pm for example.
- Challenge yourself to find ways around the barriers you put up as to why you can't do something. Think creatively or talk to someone else who can offer a different perspective
- Keep observing your thoughts as they come into your mind; as any judgemental thoughts arise, notice them and let them pass through without engaging with them
- Create your plan with full attention and awareness of your thinking and feeling

During the working day

Your work-life balance depends on your ability to make the right choices of what to engage in on a moment by moment basis during the working day. These choices, if made mindfully, will allow you to act with consciousness based on what's important and urgent rather than just drifting into the next item on the to-do list or the next meeting in the diary. Mindful pauses will allow you to be more responsive and proactive rather than just reacting without consideration for the implications.

If you want to improve your work-life balance, you will have to make some changes in line with the vision you have set for yourself. This may mean stopping doing things or doing things differently, delegating or challenging yourself or others. The important thing is to do these things with mindful awareness.

Switching off at the end of the day

Some people carry on working long after they have left their place of work and sometimes this is habit-driven; sometimes it's an inability to switch off; sometimes it may be a conscious decision. This work may be in the form of checking emails, phone calls, reading work related papers, completing paperwork or simply just mulling over work related issues or tasks to be done in your own head. The issue here is the extent to which your decision is a conscious one, made with awareness of the impact it has on you and your partner/family – if your working is habitual or you are struggling to switch off, the following may help:

Make a conscious decision when you are going to shift your focus from work to home. Is it the moment you step out of the workplace? At a point on the journey home? As you open the door to your home? After you have chatted through your day with your partner? At 7pm?

Once you have made the decision to draw a line under work, it can be a great time to mark the transition with a short mindful meditative practice, depending on what you are doing at the time. It might be mindful walking/driving or a meditation practice if you are on public transport where you gently shut your eyes and focus on your breathing. If work thoughts intrude, escort them gently out of the way and re-focus on your walking/driving/breathing. Or it may be you arrive home and have a mindful cup of tea or coffee or immerse yourself in playing with or talking to your children.

If thoughts or feelings about work crop up or indeed, thoughts or feelings about you in work (e.g. 'I feel so guilty I left at 6pm today' or 'I can't believe how badly that presentation went') then it's time to focus mindfully on whatever you are doing and allow those thoughts to be released with a sense of self-compassion. It's important to be able to process such thoughts and learn from them and it's also important that the thinking happens at a time of your choosing, rather than when the thoughts emerge. This ensures a mindful approach that is more likely to lead to problem-solving than rumination, which is likely to lead to feelings of inadequacy and anxiety.

Getting a good night's sleep

Thoughts and feelings about work are no respecters of bedtime and can be unwelcome intruders in the early hours. It may be helpful to practice a short mediation once you are in your bed before you go to sleep and if you wake in the night.

Be aware of your body and the support of the bed. Breathe in and out slowly and relax all parts of your body. Scan through the different parts of the body, starting with the head and ending with your toes. Do this slowly and gently, noting any distractions and then returning your focus to the next part of your body. This is a shortened version of the body scan meditation. See Appendix (Page 119) for more details. If thoughts intrude, you could mentally tell yourself, 'let go' and focus again on the body touching the bed. It may be helpful to focus your thoughts on a phrase e.g. 'I breathe out' on the out-breath and 'I breathe in' on the in-breath. Once you have scanned the body, return to focusing on your breathing and noticing carefully how your body moves in response to the breath.

It's hard to get perfect work life balance all of the time – sometimes, acceptance is what's needed most, combined with self-compassion and the reassurance that you are doing your best. Some things are outside of your control; some things are within your control. Being mindful of the difference will help you invest your energy wisely.

Summary

- **Determine a realistic goal for balance in your life and commit**
- **Make moment-by moment choices that support your goal**
- **Bring awareness to your thinking/feeling/actions**
- **Practice mindfulness during any awake moments during the night**

Conclusion

The whole premise of the book is to encourage you to think more about how you go through the working day so that you can do so better prepared to respond to changes, opportunities and challenges.

Even if you've done nothing more than read this book, we hope you will have picked up some handy tips to improve your wellbeing, relationships and performance at work.

If you have read the book, practiced the mindfulness techniques and used some of the good practice suggestions, we sincerely hope that your experience of working life is now more positive and productive than it was before you started.

It may be somewhat counterintuitive in this fast-paced world to suggest being more thoughtful around how we approach each moment of the day. Throughout the book, we often suggest pausing, breathing and noticing thoughts, feelings. Perhaps it does take a little longer. And perhaps this is exactly what we need to feel more resourceful, more resilient, less rushed, less stressed. Pause, tune in, check your thoughts and feelings and respond appropriately.

We all have times when we fail to do this; when we react emotionally, when we forget things because our minds are so full, when we miss what's going on because we're not giving things our full attention. As you start to practice a more mindful approach to working life, these things are still likely to happen. Hopefully you will be less judgemental of yourself than you might have been in the past. After all, being mindful is about noticing things, without judgement, to enable greater acceptance. It doesn't mean you can't change things in the future. It just means that you bring compassion to yourself rather than criticism for what you think, how you feel, or what you do.

There are three important attitudes we would like to share with you that you can bring to mindfulness to help you gain the most value from the practice:

- **Set the intention** to have a daily or regular practice. What has brought you to choose this book? What are you wanting to achieve? Steven Covey in '7 Habits of Highly Effective People' says that Habits are formed from practice and that leads to the second attitude:

114

- **Practice is essential!** The patterns of mind that we will be working to change have often been around for a long time. These patterns are often habitual and automatic. We can only expect to succeed in making changes in these long established ways of mind if we put time and effort into learning new ways. It can be time consuming and a big commitment to do these practices. Mindfulness is a simple concept but far from easy. And it is a practice.

- Thirdly, **bring a beginners mind** with you to the practice. With a beginners mind we are open to the possibility of everything and our learning is deeper as we have an attitude of curiosity and willingness to explore and play with ideas within the boundaries that we set for ourselves.

As you continue to practice a more mindful approach to working life, the times when you experience the negative aspects of mindlessness are likely to lessen. You will start to notice the benefits of mindfulness and colleagues will start to notice. We hope that family and friends and contacts outside of work will also notice the difference.

How much might your life improve all round if you were mindful in more aspects of everything you do on a daily basis? What impact might mindfulness have on how you choose to spend your time? How you engage with your family? How you eat? How you drive?

There's no reason why you can't adapt some of the exercises in the book to non-work situations. Simply pause and bring your full awareness and attention to the present moment. Notice what's going on. Really notice. Now keep that level of awareness as you choose how to proceed.

As you start to develop your ability to be more mindful, chances are you will notice that other people may also benefit from this approach. How might you help them?

Mindfulness is often learned in a group setting as it can be helpful to be able to talk through your experiences of the practices and indeed putting things into practice with others. There are mindfulness teachers (ourselves included) who can put on sessions for you and your colleagues in the workplace. If you would like more information on this, please see www.themindfulapproach.com for more information.

Appendix of mindfulness practices

Ten breaths

It can be as simple as taking ten breaths; really notice the in breath coming into your body and the out breath leaving your body. Your focus is exclusively on following the path of the breath for the duration of the in breath and the duration of the out breath for the count of ten breaths. Allow any thoughts that pop up to drift away as the focus is gently and non-judgementally turned back to the breath.

Basic breath practice

Count slowly to five as you inhale. Hold your breath for a count to three. Exhale for a count of eight.

Box breathing

Imagine in your mind you can visualise a box with four sides.

Breathe in for four seconds as you follow the top of the box.

Hold your breath for four seconds as you travel down the right side of the box.

Breathe out for four seconds as you travel along the bottom line of the box.

Hold your breath for four seconds as you travel up the left hand side of the box.

Repeat for four or more cycles.

One minute meditation

The first time you carry out this practice, set a timer for one minute so that you can count the number of breaths you typically take in a minute.

Sit comfortably, relaxed, upright, with your feet flat on the floor, hands on your abdomen.

Close your eyes or lower your gaze. Just breathe, inhaling and exhaling at your own pace.

Don't force the breath, just breathe however you normally breathe, counting at the end of each out breath.

Once you know how many breaths you take in a minute, you can simply spend a minute breathing and focusing on the breath whenever you need, quite literally, to take a breather.

Three step breathing space

Sit in your chair, feet flat on the floor, sitting slightly forward in an upright, alert yet relaxed position. Relax your hands in your lap. Close your eyes gently if you feel comfortable doing so. If not, lower your gaze and look downwards. Take a couple of deep breaths as you settle and bring your attention to your body and your awareness of what's going on inside you right now.

What thoughts are going through your mind? Notice your thinking and simply label it 'thinking' rather than getting caught up in the thoughts themselves.

Ask 'what feelings are here?' Notice those feelings; don't get caught up in those feelings or try to change them.

Ask 'What body sensations are here right now?' Scan the body to notice any feelings, from your feet, through your legs, though your stomach, waist, chest, your arms, your neck and your head. Just notice the sensations in your body.

Now bring your attention to the breath. Notice how the breath comes in and out of the body, how your stomach rises and falls. Notice breathing in and breathing out. Follow the breath all the way in and all the way out. Use each breath as an opportunity to anchor yourself into the present. If the mind wanders, gently escort the attention back to the breath. Breathing in and breathing out.

Notice your feet on the floor. Notice how the chair feels against your body. Notice what's going on around you – any sounds and smells. Focus on the whole body, right here, right now. Be aware of the whole body, moment by moment. If your mind wanders, bring it back to awareness of your body. Relax into your body and very gently bring your awareness back into the room, opening your eyes when you are ready and notice how you feel right now. Be aware of how the breathing space has impacted you, whatever that impact may be.

Even a single, conscious breath, with focus and intention can enable you to pause in the moment, take stock and carry on with your day in a more mindful way.

Ten minutes breathing

Find ten minutes to sit quietly in a chair with your back away from the back of the chair, your body upright and your feet flat on the floor. Start by noticing the contact points of your body with the chair and the floor. Is there any tension around your shoulders? Allow your shoulders to relax and begin by turning your attention to the rhythm of your breathing, just noticing how fast or slow your breathing is; where your breath is most noticeable to you right now. Is it in the rise or fall of your belly as you breathe in and out? Or the rise and fall of your chest or perhaps at your nostrils? Wherever your breathing is most noticeable for you start to focus your attention on the in breath entering your body and the out breath leaving your body. Don't try to control your breath, you only need to follow the path of your breath in and out of your body and be curious about what you can notice about your breathing. Thoughts will come into your mind, just notice these thoughts and let them go, perhaps making a mental note of that particular thought so that you can return to it later, after the meditation.

The body scan

You can do this lying down or sitting up.

Remind yourselves that this is a time for being awake, rather than falling asleep.

Close your eyes and bring your awareness to the sensations in your abdomen, as you breathe in and out and as your abdomen rises and falls.

Take your attention, as if it was a spotlight, and bring it down your body into your legs, into both feet and all the way out to your toes.

Focus on each of your toes, with a gentle interested attention. Become aware of any sensations. Maybe you notice the feeling of contact between your toes, a tingling sensation, warmth or numbness or no sensation at all.

Whatever you experience is OK. There is no need to judge. Don't change anything, just let the sensations be just as they are.

On the in breath imagine that the air can enter the lungs and travel all the way down the body, through your legs and into your toes. On the out breath, feel or imagine the air flowing out of the toes, the feet and your torso and out of your nose. Take a few breaths, imagining the passage of air down to your toes and up again and out through your nose.

When you are ready let go of the toes and bring your awareness to the bottom of your feet, to the instep, your heel, noticing any sensations; as you become aware of sensations, breathe into them using the in breath to gently bring awareness into the sensations and notice how, if at all, those sensations change as you breath out of them.

Bring your awareness to the top of your feet, into the ankles. On an out breath let go of your feet and bring your attention to your lower legs, to the shins and calves noticing sensations in the skin and below the surface. Move your attention up to your knees and then your thighs, across your pelvic areas.

If your mind wanders, as it will do, make a mental note of where your mind wandered to and gently return your awareness to the part of the body you are focusing on.

Become aware of your lower back, abdomen, upper back, your chest noticing your heart beating and your lungs filling with each in breath. As you breathe out, turn your focus to your shoulders, a key place for holding stress; notice how your shoulders feel, breathe into any discomfort.

Gently bring your awareness into both hands, the sensations in the tips of your fingers and thumbs and then your whole fingers and thumbs, the palms of your hands and the backs of your hands, then gently move up to your wrists, lower arms and elbows, shoulders and armpits. Be aware of your neck, your face, jaw, mouth, lips, nose, cheeks, ears, eyes and forehead and finally your entire head.

Finally cast your mind over your entire body and feel the sensations of wholeness, feeling the breath flowing in and out of your body.

This exercise can take just a few minutes, or be extended as required.

Eating meditations

Find something small to eat like a grape, sultana, slice of fruit, or a piece of chocolate. Still the mind and tune into your breath as you bring all of your attention to the piece of food in your hand looking at it as if you are a child seeing this piece of food for the very first time. What can you notice about it? Explore and be curious about the textures; shades; colours; shapes; the weight and feel. Touch it; smell it; listen to it; place it in your mouth and see what you notice about how your body responds, your thoughts and your feelings; bite into the food and pay attention to your senses. Finally, slowly chew the food noticing as much detail as possible in your response to the act of eating this food.

During a coffee break or a lunch break, take time to really notice the smells, flavours and tastes of what you are eating and drinking.

Mindfulness of sound

Sitting in stillness, aware of the flow of your breath into and out of your body; gently bring your attention to the sounds around you. Hear the sounds without labelling them; Listen to the space between the sounds as well as the sounds themselves; notice how far in the distance you can hear sounds. Each time your mind drifts away gently bring it back to noticing the sounds.

Mindful walking

At any point before, during or after the working day, you have the opportunity to walk mindfully and focus on your body moving; the experience of being 'in your body' as opposed to being 'in your head' can be calming and grounding. Notice the pressure of your feet on the ground. Feel the sensations as your weight shifts from foot to foot. Tune into all your senses as you move and notice any thinking without engaging with it. You can say to yourself, 'just walking' as a reminder that your focus is not your mind, but your body.

Mindfulness of nature

Take time to walk in nature and as you walk open your senses to what is here now. Be aware of your breath; be aware of your thoughts without being caught in the thought and gently and with curiosity view your environment, the colours, shapes, noises, smells, temperature, feelings inside your body and on your skin.

Catherine was first introduced to meditation in a cave in Thailand in 1991. Her first experience of meditation in the workplace was in the late 1990s when working as a training consultant. Meditation was used as a team development tool to enable trust, understanding and dialogue amongst the team members. In 2003, Catherine set up her own development consultancy, providing management development workshops and executive coaching. Catherine started to practice mindfulness and, in time, introduced this concept to certain clients, realising that it was a remarkable way of managing stressful situations at work. Catherine is trained in Workplace MT (Workplace Mindfulness Training) and works as an executive coach and workshop facilitator, incorporating mindfulness into her work and life.

Catherine can be contacted through www.thepositiveapproach.co.uk and www.themindfulapproach.com

Carroll has worked in several senior positions in blue chip organisations in the UK and Europe, including working at board level. As a coach and workshop facilitator for over 20 years, Carroll has worked to bring about transformational change at a one to one; team; corporate and organisational level. Trained as a psychotherapist, Carroll has creative insight into the impact that complexity, the pace of change and uncertainty has on leaders and managers. Looking for tools to help clients deal with the reality of today's workplace led Carroll to training as a mindfulness teacher at the Centre for Mindfulness at Bangor University and the Oxford Centre for Mindfulness. Carroll combines her background and experience in business, psychotherapy and mindfulness into her work with managers and leaders, developing their capacity to operate at their best more often.

Carroll can be contacted through www.themindfulapproach.com and www.cm2c.com.